The Book of Life
Lessons from Mother Earth

Channelled and written

by

Victoria Cochrane M.Ed. (Hons)
Psychic Communicator and Spiritual Healer

The Book of Life: Lessons from Mother Earth
Author: Victoria Cochrane
Copyright © 2020 Victoria Cochrane
Tasmania, Australia
ABN: 58 759 564 318
Category: New Age Publications; Ascension; Mother Earth; Spirituality

All rights reserved. This book may not be reproduced in whole or in part. stored or posted without express permission from the author and publisher of this book.

Cover by Renea Stubbs.
Editing and Foreword by Kelli Parker.
Recorded meditation formatting by Gary Martin.
Meditation Music by Christopher Lloyd Clarke, Enlightened Audio.
Book formatted and published by Synk Media.
Printed by Synk Media and on demand in Australia, United States and United Kingdom.

Victoria Cochrane, 1960 –
Website: victoriacochrane.com.au
Email: victoriacochrane44@gmail.com

ISBN: 978-0-646-81915-0 (e-book)
       978-0-646-81916-7 (print)

Dedications

To all who are struggling
to find joy in your lives,
may this book re-inspire,
re-invigorate and re-new you.

May it raise your vibrations,
and thus your consciousness,
to a higher frequency
and, above all, help you
to see life as a gift.

Blessings,
Victoria xx

To beautiful Bobbie Mae,
May the world be your oyster
and your life full of joy,
laughter and endless love.

Nanna 'Tor

Contents

Foreword	i
About this Book	iii
Grounding & Connecting: Stay Safe While Meditating	v

Awakening to Your Divine Blueprint — 1

The Journey to Oneness	3
Connect to the Light of Creation	5
The Violet Flame of Transmutation: The Greatest Gift to the World	7
Invoke the Violet Flame of Transmutation	10
The Escalating Energies of Ascension	13
Lightbody Ascension Activation	18
The Art of Waking Consciousness	21
Connect to Your Higher Mind	25
Unlocking the Codes of Creation	27
Create a Positive Belief System Around Abundance	29
Unlocking Your Inner Wisdom	33
Connect to Your Psychic Gifts	37
Karmic and Soul Family Contracts	39
Clear the Soul of Past Life Trauma and Resolve Karmic Debt	45
The Spirit of God	47
Connect to the Unconditional Love of Source	50
The Human Collective Consciousness	53
Heal Your Bodies and Energy Fields	55

The Gift of Life on Earth: Connecting to the Elements of Nature — 57

The Love of Mother Earth	59
Healing for Mother Earth	62
The Magic of Life	65
Connect to Nature	68
The Patterns of Life	71
Transmute Pollutants and Greenhouse Gasses	74

Trees: Earth's Natural Protectors   77
Ground to Mother Earth   *80*

Water: The Flow of Life   83
Connect to the River of Life   *87*

Mountains: The Stillpoint of Creation   89
Stillpoint Meditation   *92*

Crystals: Energy Healers   95
Crystal Healing Meditations   *98*

The Insect Kingdom: Bees –
Working Together for the Greater Good of All   101
Reharmonize the Body Using a Pendulum   *104*

The Animal Kingdom: 107
Mammals – Unconditional Love   107
The Sacred Breath   *111*

As Free as a Bird   115
Rebuild Self-Love and Feelings of Worthiness   *119*

A Bird's Eye View of Climate Change   121
Send Healing Energy to the Planet and Humanity   *124*

Embodying Your Spirituality   **127**

The Attack on the World   129
Absolve Fear Stemming from the Third Dimension   *133*

Regaining Your Voice   135
Meditate for Inner Peace   *138*

The 11:11 Ascension Portal   141
Enter the Ascension Portal   *144*

The Colours of the Ascension of Humanity   147
Align to the Rays of Ascension   *150*

The Power of Meditation   153
A Warm Hug Meditation   *156*

Take Back Your Power and Embrace Your Mastery   159

A Final Word   163
Credits   166
About the Author   167
Other Titles by Victoria Cochrane   168

Foreword

Victoria and I met in 2007 at an Australian Literacy Educators Association Conference. She was an experienced teacher and I a student almost finished my teaching degree. We shared a conversation as we ate our lunch. A few weeks later I was door knocking for the Heart Foundation in my street and knocked on her door. She invited me in and we again had another conversation. Living in the same street, teaching and sharing a passion for literacy education saw us become fast friends. We were even lucky enough to work together in the same school for a year before she decided to move back to the North West of Tasmania.

I have watched her gifts grow in strength and her confidence in her own psychic abilities grow along with them. I feel truly blessed to have her in my life and to be able to call her my friend. She crossed my path for a reason and I have learned many things from her. Her gifts have helped me make sense of happenings in my life many times. She loves unconditionally, is loved unconditionally and I am so proud of her.

This, her fourth book, is one I see myself returning to over and over. There is so much knowledge in here to absorb and learn from. I love the meditations at the end of each chapter and how they will assist the reader to assimilate the knowledge into action and their lives. Tor has cleared me, healed me, lifted past trauma, taught me to trust my own intuition, how to meditate, protect myself and given me the greatest gift, her friendship for which I thank her.

She has much to teach us all and seeks to help others live their best lives while on the road to mastery. Love is always the way.

Kelli Parker, 2020

About this Book

This book began as a gift to me from the Creator. While I was in a Theta state in the Seventh Plane, one day in 2017, the Creator handed me a book called "The Book of Life." It was like one of those 3D children's books where the images have several levels and are kind of holographic, but the really special thing about this ethereal book was that I could enter into it and be a part of the beautiful pictures.

The first chapter contained a picture of trees, the next, oceans and the next was mountains. I spent a few months exploring each one when I had the time. After about a year, however, I expanded my channellings beyond the book and created my own "Book of Life," spring-boarding off the original ideas presented by the Creator and incorporating many of the channellings I had stored on my computer that were a good fit for the theme of this book. Some of the topics are similar to those in my other three books, but the messages are now deeper and more expansive; it seemed important for me to include them. It also seemed a logical idea to include a meditation with each chapter to assist readers to experience the beauty of each chapter, or to clear blockages that may have become apparent whilst reading.

I want to thank the Creator and the masters of the Cosmic Council for assisting me to bring the information and meditations through. Although the messages do not come from me persay, they resonate so much with my soul and I totally trust the truths held within them.

I hope you enjoy this book as much as I have enjoyed bringing it to you.

Victoria Cochrane, 2020

Meditations

Grounding & Connecting: Stay Safe While Meditating

Most meditations in this book start with a comprehensive guide to relaxing, grounding and connecting. It is important to me that people using my meditations have a beautiful experience, so please take the time to connect to the light and be protected during each meditation.

The basic guide is outlined for you here:

> *Sit or lie in a quiet place. Close your eyes and breathe your energy deep into Mother Earth, then bring it back up through your chakras and all the way to your crown. Sit your energy in your light at the top of your crown if you can, otherwise focus your attention on it. You will see a beam of light extending through your body and up above it; this light connects you to the Source of Creation, the Creator of All That Is and protects you from absorbing lower energies. Hold the intention that you are connected to the Creator's light and protected throughout your meditation.*

Blessings,
Victoria

Part 1

Awakening to Your Divine Blueprint

Chapter 1
The Journey to Oneness

The breath of life comes from all things, because everything on Earth is one with the Supreme Creator. Religions on Earth teach that man is separate from and lesser than the Creator, or God, but that is a fallacy and a myth. All living beings and non-living things are spokes of the Divine wheel and are therefore one with the Divine Source. Humans are co-creators, because they create their own reality with every thought, word, action and every decision that they make. Creation, Dear Hearts, is in every one of you and in every natural particle on Earth. God is you and you are God.

Oneness means that all things in the Universe are connected by infinite threads and that there is no separation between them. The knowledge of oneness brings awareness of self as a spiritual, etheric being who is infinitely connected with and loved unconditionally by the Creator. When you know you are one with the Creator, you feel loved unconditionally in all areas of your life and will give it to others in equal measure; there is no judgement or condemnation, only love and light. To achieve Oneness you need do nothing, for it is already so! To live your life in full awareness of Oneness, however, is another matter.

To live in Oneness is to live in a fifth-dimensional state at all times; in the denseness of third dimensional Earth, this is no mean feat and is difficult to sustain without continued awareness and vigilance. Only those who have managed to bring in their lightbodies and to raise their vibrations above the drama and chaos of life on Earth are able, for the most part, to stay in an ascended state and to help others to reach it.

Any dimensional state is a vibrational frequency aligned to a certain consciousness. The higher the frequency the higher the dimension that the person will be operating consciously in. All dimensions are light infused, and if the frequency of light is low, the vibration will also be low, meaning that, at a conscious level, the person or being is likely to be egotistical and self-absorbed. The more light that one allows into their chakras through the clearing of blockages, such as past emotional abuse or trauma, the higher their consciousness will become, thus entering a higher dimensional state. This will result in the person being less in ego and more able to see things from another person's point of view. The raising of one's consciousness to a state of Oneness does not happen overnight, nor can one stay in the Fifth Dimension without concerted effort and awareness of one's thoughts, perceptions and attitudes towards self and others. Ascension is always a work in progress and is also not a linear process.

The light of the Creator is of the highest frequency because it is that of unconditional love; there is no higher state than this. To connect to the Creator as a matter of course is to bring oneself into alignment with his light and the fifth dimensional state of Oneness. As one practices connection to Source and revels in the unconditional loving energy, one will begin to release the traumas of the past and to become one with his breath, his soul, his essence and his light. When one knows how this energy feels, the urge to continue the journey of reconnection to one's own divinity will be self-perpetuating, continuing the awakening until the person themselves becomes the light for others who are still finding their way. This is the way of Ascension, coming in waves of awakening until all humans who choose this path will determine the vibration of humanity, rising above the Third Dimension and bringing the Earth fully into the New Age.

Bring in the light of the Creator, Dear Hearts, into your heart space, into your breath and into your being. Hold his light as love and feel it as your love, for the love of the Creator is also your own. Know that the love of the Creator lives and breathes in all things and there is nothing that is separate from him or that is not loved by him. When you know the unconditional love of the Creator and live within His light, you will also see everything from a place of love. One cannot judge others when one lives in the light and love of the Creator, nor can one judge oneself, because the Creator knows no such state.

Love is all there is, and that is all.

And so it is.

Chapter 1

Meditation One
Connect to the Light of Creation

Sit quietly in your body until your breathing is slow and regular and you feel calm and relaxed. Breathe in, breathe out. Breathe in, breathe out. Focus your attention on your heartspace and fill the area with light. When the energy is a beautiful ball of light in the centre of your chest, take a breath and send it as a beam of light down through your chakras, through your legs and down through your feet to ground into Mother Earth. See, feel or imagine light roots anchoring you into the earth then, on several inbreaths, bring the beam of energy back up through your body until it is rotating above your crown.

See, feel or imagine the light connecting to all of your chakras below it and above it, reaching up to a huge ball of sparkly light that is the same as your own. Holding the intention that you are connected in Oneness with the Source of Creation see, feel or imagine your ball of light merging together with all of your chakras into the light of Creation, becoming one. Breathing steadily in and out and focusing on the light, relax your body and clear your mind, focusing only on your breath and the feeling of being one with the unconditional love of the Source of Creation.

Feel the energy change as you are immersed in the blissful feeling of peace, love and truth. Allow the light to penetrate every cell of your body and part of your being, healing and rebalancing you. If you wish, ask a question, give thanks for something or someone in your life or just be. Be careful to be specific and positive with your thoughts, as this is the ultimate energy for manifestation.

When you are ready, breathe your energy back down into your crown, knowing you are still connected to the unconditional love of Source and protected from lower or toxic energies. Bring your energy back into your heartspace and open your eyes.

I AM the Creator of All That Is

Chapter 2
The Violet Flame of Transmutation: The Greatest Gift to the World

As Mother Earth continues to weather the storm of Ascension in the duality of the 3rd Dimension, the Human Collective Consciousness fluctuates wildly between the darkest negativity and the highest vibration of unconditional love. Humans who are sensitive to the energy of others are finding that they can be joyous in mood one day then desperately depressed the other. For many, finding an equilibrium in the disorganised and unpredictable mix of discordant/violent/love energy circling the globe is an impossible task. For the awakened and enlightened, the powers of the Violet Flame of Transmutation are an absolute necessity if they are to continue their work of helping others to raise their vibrations and consciousness out of the mire that is the 3rd Dimension.

Amongst the masses, the Violet Flame is unknown and untouched, yet in Wayshowers' and Lightworkers' circles the Violet Flame is an important tool for the survival of humanity. When the Violet Flame is called upon, it will instantly transmute any negative emotions, feelings and vibrations into love. The sparks of golden light signalling the transmutation are automatically sent out to the world, creating a love vibration that resonates with that of Mother Earth. Because the flame comes from and is one with the Earth, the effects upon Mother Earth are immediate, causing a ripple effect that goes far beyond the area where transmutation occurred.

The Violet Flame is of the Seventh Ray, which is the overlighting ray of the Age of Aquarius, and is radiated by Archangel Zadkiel and his Archeia, Holy Amethyst. As the name suggests, the amethyst crystal is associated with the Violet Flame and is used by crystal healers to absorb and transmute negative energies in the home and in personal or sacred spaces. The colour violet is that of the crown chakra and the seventh ray and is therefore the highest healing colour in the spectrum. When used consciously by humans to transmute toxic feelings of hatred, anger, resentment, jealousy, depression and spite, the positive effects on personal relationships, on negative workspaces and on collective or group consciousness are noticeable and far-reaching.

The Violet Flame contains light codes that are of a much higher vibration than that of ordinary light, because it is infused with the 7th ray, which is divine in nature and connected to the Oneness of the All. The codes override the lower vibrations of all other colours in the spectrum, instantly transmuting all negativity to unconditional love. The effects on the energy that the flame transmutes is instantaneous, producing a shift in vibration that lifts feelings, temperament and emotions out of anger and fear to a higher frequency, allowing people to feel calmer, less anxious and more in harmony with the world and each other. The light codes are instantly adaptable within changing dimensions of consciousness and gradients of light, making this ethereal flame a true gift to the world.

Many people who are awakening are using and invoking the flame through masters of light, but many are also astounded to find the flame emanating through their own crowns. The flame is not exclusive – there are no chosen few who can access its powers. When one has opened their crown chakra and accepted their connection to the highest source, the Creator of All That Is, along with holding the loving intention of serving the world in their own way without ego or the need for sacrifice, the flame becomes a part of their energy and is always accessible.

Light codes of any nature are energy and can change DNA structure according to their vibrational frequency. If the codes are of a low vibration, the energy of the person will be weakened allowing disease, pain, illness and emotional overload to take hold. The higher the vibration of light/energy that can enter a person's cells, the healthier the person will be. The use of the Violet Flame on the body to rid it of low vibrational feelings, emotions, toxins and even chemicals makes it an extremely powerful tool and one that has the potential to change and strengthen DNA to become resistant to disease.

As the attempts of those who wish to rule the masses with fear, terror and violence drastically increases, the daily use by lightworkers and the spiritually aware to transmute their own negative energies, as well as that in the collective consciousness, is critical to the ongoing ascension of the planet. Archangel Zadkiel/Holy Amethyst, myself and any of the masters of light can be called upon at any time to assist you to call up the Violet Flame whenever the need arises. We urge you to be proactive in this cause.

I AM Saint Germain (Sanctus Germanis).

Meditation Two
Invoke the Violet Flame of Transmutation

Take three deep and relaxing breaths, feeling yourself present in the space. Intend that you are grounded into Mother Earth as you focus your intention on your breath, bringing it to a steady count of four breaths in and four breaths out. Connect now to your Higher Self by envisioning a golden light coming through your crown, spreading through your mind and connecting through your heartspace, then going all the way down your chakra line. Focusing on your heartspace see, feel or imagine a beautiful, pink lotus flower forming in front of you, unfolding its petals and growing larger and more luminous. It slowly comes towards you, entering your heartspace and filling you with the most wonderful feeling of bliss, joy and peace.

Now become aware of Archangel Zadkiel as he invokes the Violet Flame of Transmutation, bringing it up from under your feet until it surrounds you and fills your bodies, chakras, organs, cells and aura. He invites you to let go of any negative thoughts or emotions you may have been holding towards yourself and others and to release them into the flame. As you consciously let go of these thoughts and emotions, see them spark off as golden light. Continue releasing until you feel a shift of energy within your physical body.

When you are ready, allow the flame to subside and the pink light of the lotus to fill the spaces left behind. Say now to yourself: "I love and accept myself. I allow myself to be loved and accepted. I AM love, I AM loved, I AM." As you say these words, an incredible feeling of love fills your body and radiates out to every cell, filling every corner of your being and raising your vibration to a higher dimension.

Watch now as the lotus flower turns to white while the centre is slowly filled with pink light. Continue breathing in and out on a slow count of four until you feel completely calm, at peace and filled with the light and love of the Creator of All-That-Is. Hold the energy until you feel that the healing is finished. Give thanks and gratitude to Archangel Zadkiel then, when you are ready, count backwards from 10 to 1 and open your eyes.

I AM Yeshua ben Yoseph (Jesus).

Chapter 3
The Escalating Energies of Ascension

The energies of Ascension have been active well before 2012 and have been accelerating ever since. The awakening of human consciousness has increased world-wide awareness of corruption and the hidden agendas of those in power, which has resulted in the fall from grace of many political and high-profile figures to date. The most recent uprising has been against corruption and paedophilia in the Roman Catholic Church, which has showcased the many failings of doctrine that flies in the face of basic human rights. Acts of terrorism, travesties of war against innocent humans and single, often random acts of violence have increased, so much so that many souls have decided they have had enough and are leaving the planet in droves to escape from the harsh realities of life on Earth, in the form of sudden deaths by suicide, illness or accidents,

The amount of energy currently being downloaded (and yet to come), along with its intensity and height of vibration, has the potential to 'knock people for a six' if they are not in the process of bringing in their Lightbodies, or if their energies have become dense. Maintaining connection to the Creator's light and bringing it into their being, staying grounded and diligently protecting their energies is recommended to those who spend a lot of time in other people's energy fields. If you are one of those people, it is crucial for you to be vigilant in your protection and clearing regimes.

Many people are now wondering whether the shifting energies will begin to slow down in the beginning of the next decade from 2020, but this will not be the case. If anything, the energy of Ascension will increase and any changes that have been in the wind will manifest in full force. One cannot ascend into the Fifth Dimension without at first shedding past hurts, fears and emotions, and for those who have been resisting the need to face the past and embrace change, the world will seem as if it is crashing down upon them. Change is better embraced, however, because it is an opportunity to finally let go of the past and all that keeps one static. Anyone who can do that will then be able to look to the present and the future to fully move on. Those who have, on the other hand, embraced the energies and raised their vibrations will find others coming to them to ask for assistance and advice.

Lightworkers and wayshowers began their ascension process early so they could be bridges for those awakening in the future. Ascension, for those who are unaware, is the process of raising one's vibrations and consciousness to a level higher than the masses to one of patience, tolerance, acceptance and love. To do this, one's chakras must accept light codes and frequencies that can cause physical disequilibrium for a time. The process can be considerably slowed if a person's chakras are clogged with past or present emotional grief, trauma or negative belief systems or the physical body heavy with chemicals and toxins.

Humans must accept that the ascension of the Earth is very real and take the opportunity now to shed their ego to begin the process of stepping into their soul's purpose for reincarnating on the Earth. They must let go of past hurts and trauma and embrace the unconditional love of the Creator as their birthright. If it is happening to you but you are unsure how to harness it, seek out a wayshower who has already travelled that path. This is part of their soul purpose and they will be able to guide you.

There are millions of people around the world awakening to the fact that the only saviour of the world is love and the only people they can work on is themselves. As more and more people begin to find their own spirituality outside of doctrine and religion, the more light goes out to the world and mingles with the darkness. The resulting conflict of light and dark is bringing much instability to the weather as well as to mass human emotions causing the collective consciousness to constantly fluctuate between polars of negativity and positivity. On the Earthly Plane, this equates to escalating violence amongst humans, unpredictable weather patterns, an increase in the number of catastrophes around the planet and an unprecedented number of deaths. It also means that, as the veil lifts and more people wake up and begin to raise their consciousness, more and more lies and untruths of people in power are being revealed. No longer can those who have gained power at the expense of others hide behind illusion and glamour; as the façade falls away, there will be many more falls from grace yet.

Consider this: at the time of your death, what can you take with you? If you looked back on your life, what would you hold in your heart to treasure in the afterlife? It doesn't take much to realise that what is most important in life is not material or solid and cannot be bought. If you died tomorrow, would you leave with love in your heart and integrity in your soul? Would you be remembered with love and heartache, or relief that you were no longer around?

The way you live your life is what you take with you, Dear Hearts, and the imprint you leave on the Earth can impact the people you knew for a long time. What does this mean? Considering that every thought word and deed connect to the human collective consciousness, it is a poignant reminder that people who pass over are remembered by people who loved or despised them. The way they are remembered also affects the collective consciousness, so the legacy you leave will continue affecting the world well after you have departed this life. Will you be remembered with remorse, hatred and ill-feeling, or will you be discussed with loving words and fond thoughts?

If you are honest with yourself in reflection and you come to the conclusion that there is work to be done on your disposition to decrease the negativity you emit to the world, the first step is to consider why you may be a 'glass-half-empty' person in some instances. To do so will give you the chance to start changing the things that are within your control, that being your thoughts, the words you use with each person you interact with and your judgement of yourself and others. The first positive change you can make today is to stop yourself from thinking or speaking about yourself or others in a negative manner and to immediately reword your words or thoughts in a more positive frame.

The state of peoples' minds on Earth affects everything that happens there, from minor accidents, flares of temper and violence, to the catastrophic changes in the weather. All in the Universe is united in thought, word and deed and nothing can be unaffected by the actions, thoughts or words of any individual on any planet in any galaxy in the Universe. Every action has an equal and opposite reaction and, as the pendulum swings one way, so it must reverse its action and return. As the saying goes, what you give out will come back to you. If you are violent and angry, the reactions from others back to you will be the same. If you are loving and friendly, people will return the emotions, even if they started out feeling differently. This is called the Law of Attraction and it is one of the three major laws governing the Universe.

Every considered or unchecked thought is an energy that spirals out to the atmosphere, mingling with every other thought from every other human on Earth, creating a mass of consciousness that cannot be seen, but of which the reverberations affect every living and non-loving thing on Earth and beyond. If it is predominantly positive, the effects will be equally as positive. However, (as is deliberately magnified in the media), the predominance of negative emotions in the collective consciousness can be felt by people around the world, producing reactions around the globe as war, terrorism, fire, floods and earthquakes, resulting in a mass exodus of souls from the planet. Those in power, or those who have influence over them, who wish to keep the masses controlled through fear and intimidation, are fighting a losing battle however, as the media also works against them! Just as fake news is spread through the media, so is the truth; the more lies that are spread the more likely the truth will be revealed. This is because a mass awakening is occurring around the world, as souls become more in tune with their spiritual paths and become less able to be duped. Yes, the wool is falling off the eyes of the masses and Ascension is occurring, despite the best efforts of those working to keep the energies of the Third Dimension in place.

The most important thing to remember is that you are all made in God's image and that very image is unconditional love. When humans speak and act in the vibration of love, the Earth will respond in kind; letting go of ego and seeing each other and the world through your Sacred Heart will bring about changes that could be truly wondrous. For many people it is already happening, as they open their consciousness to the higher perspective of their Christed-selves. To see through the lens of love is to be able to accept that differences are all part of the same Divine wheel, making up the one true God - the Supreme Source, the Creator of All That Is. To believe that is to accept that there is no separation of any man, woman or child that makes them any different, less important or any less connected to the Creator than any other human. The vibration of unconditional love is one of total acceptance, tolerance and equality for all in the energy of The ALL.

When you live in the vibration of love you will receive it back in equal measure. It may not come from those to whom it was directed, but it will come. The difference one person can make to the vibrations of the world would astound you, as no measure can be made of the impact of sending unconditional love out to the world. However, if hundreds, thousands or even millions of people are aware enough to send love, even with one intentional thought, the results on the vibrational frequencies of the world will become noticeable to the human eye. Mother Earth responds to love energy through her weather patterns, the intensities of the colours in her sunrises and sunsets, the rapid regeneration of plants and animals and in the very nature of human interaction. People become much calmer and more tolerant when their surroundings are serene and beautiful. Only love can create beauty, whereas hatred and similar emotions can only create ugliness.

The vibration of love is the vibration of the Creator; it is only through love that true ascension can occur. One of the best ways to raise your vibration to that of love is through practicing gratitude and allowing forgiveness to permeate your being. Let go of the past and bring in the light. Forgive those who have transgressed upon you, including yourself if you perceive your past actions to be grievous. There is nothing in the present but love and the promise of better things to come. Now is the time to step into Mastery, claim your Divinity and bring the joy that Oneness brings to the world.

We, the Masters of Light and the Creator of All That Is are forever with you.

Meditation Three
Lightbody Ascension Activation

Breathe deeply in and out until your breathing slows to a regular count of four breaths in and four breaths out. Focus your energy, first in your heartspace then, as you relax, lower it to your abdomen. As you breathe in and out see, feel or imagine a beautiful ball of light building there. When it is strong, take a breath in and breathe it down into Mother Earth, grounding you with light roots under the ground. Then bring it all the way back up through your body, up through your crown and see, feel or imagine it connecting to the Creator's light above you. Breathing out, bring the light down around you until you see, feel or know you are surrounded and protected. Acknowledge your connection with the All and give thanks for your protection throughout this meditation.

Hold the intention, now, that the Master of Light or Archangel that is working with you comes to you to facilitate the first or continued activation of your Lightbody. See or feel their presence and give them thanks and gratitude for activating your chakras to a higher frequency of light for your highest and best. Giving them permission to begin, see or feel energy come through your aura, starting from your crown, sweeping away any unwanted attachments and repairing any tears or holes. As the energy reaches your feet, know that your chakras are also being aligned.

In the next sweep of energy from your crown, a concentrated light now permeates each chakra, working its way systematically through each chakra in order, either clearing, balancing and grounding them or, depending on how clear *they are already and how high the vibration, activating them to a higher frequency of light. When the second sweep through has finished, a third sweep of light comes in. This sweep is likely to be the strongest as, with all chakras now cleared and brought into balance, the highest activation of light can safely occur.*

See or feel the energy being swept out into your aura and your aura cleared, sealed and protected while your energies are grounded once again. If you are able, clear your mind to receive a message from the master. Give them thanks and gratitude for their service to you.

I AM Archangel Metatron

---

*Please note that you must be adequately hydrated before this meditation, which can be repeated every two or three months, depending on how quickly your consciousness is ascending.

Chapter 4
The Art of Waking Consciousness

Humans are spiritual light-beings living and learning lessons in a physical body in the third dimensional reality of planet Earth. When their body dies, their soul is released back into the light of Creation from whence they came, carrying all of the knowledge of their past existences with them. The soul carries the spirit from lifetime to lifetime, gathering wisdom, learning lessons and resolving karma until it reaches the stage of mastery, after which the soul is released from the karmic wheel. Rebirth back into a human body is thereafter a choice, not a mandate. In the 21st century, many masters of varying ages are walking the planet Earth in human form in a last-ditch attempt to bring the human consciousness to a state of oneness; in fact, all babies being born now are masters who are wise well beyond their years.

In every waking moment, human beings are consciously thinking. Their thoughts, words and actions are purposeful and deliberate, whether they are organising, planning, discussing, gossiping or writing. Underpinning these thoughts are complex belief systems that are the driving force of the intention behind every thought, spoken word and action towards other people, both kind and unkind. Conscious thought is the benefactor of both heredity and upbringing, and how a person thinks and behaves is a direct consequence of what they have learnt to believe about themselves, the world and their place in it. In sleep, however, the unconscious mind brings to the fore all of the thoughts, beliefs and doctrine stored in the recesses of the mind, playing them out in the person's dreams. The unconscious mind is also powerfully connected to the ALL and to the ethereal kingdom, to each person's spiritual guides and to their higher mind, the one that is aware of their soul contracts and spiritual purpose for reincarnation.

The conscious mind sees only what is before it and remembers physical experiences from its current reality. The sub-conscious mind, however, is in touch with the spiritual body and sees, remembers and accesses memories from other lifetimes and other worlds. It is readily able to shift from reality to reality, paradigm to paradigm, dimension to dimension, potentially leading to profound dreams and an awakening of the person's psychic abilities. This occurrence may, however, be extremely disturbing to the individual who is blocked by the physical reality of their existence, causing them to shut their minds down to the possibilities that have been shown to them. This choice to accept their Divine Blueprint is always theirs and cannot be intervened upon by anyone, human or otherwise. Accepting it can only occur when one can see beyond the physical existence on Earth and accept one's gifts. Belief systems can, in some cases, be so indoctrinated in a person, usually from a very early age, that a soul who incarnated with the intention of awakening to their own mastery can remain blocked for their entire lifetime, ultimately missing out on the opportunities available to them and on making the differences to the world that they originally came in to do.

The higher mind instinctively knows every spiritual law that binds all living souls on Earth. The unwritten laws are the guiding force of the Universe for all beings that have a conscious mind, both in body and spirit. When adhered to, everything flows in harmonious balance, but when transgressed, the disharmony causes immediate consequences that ripple out to the world and that are felt across the Universe as a whole. There are many humans transgressing many spiritual laws on a daily basis, leading them to be constantly out of balance without consciously knowing why.

The knowledge of the higher mind is often at odds with the conscious, waking mind; the feelings of unease when a spiritual law is transgressed is often a mystery to the person that is swiftly ignored, because they cannot consciously recall where or what it relates to. Those who are more spiritually awakened or who are conscious caretakers of the Earth and its environment are more likely to take notice of the signs of unease and modify their behaviour than those who are entrenched in the dense energies of third dimensional Earth.

Be assured, Dear Hearts, that each and every one of you has the knowledge of the Universe in your higher mind, including the Universal Laws. To access this knowledge, put your thinking brain out of the way, sit in your Sacred Heartspace and know with your heart, not think your mind. Trust that what comes to you is from your higher mind, as it will feel sacred and of integrity. There are many dimensions to thought, and higher-vibrational thoughts will always be underpinned with feelings of love, tolerance, understanding and peace that will bring the person into a higher waking consciousness, able to access the knowledge of their higher mind much more readily.

Your higher self is your ethereal self. It is the bridge between your physical body and the spirit world and is your portal to the ethereal kingdom. Your higher self is an aspect of a former life and may or may not be of a higher order of mastery. When you work through your higher self you have direct access to Divine energy. You will also be working between planes of existence and dimensions in time. Your higher self is not your ego, for your ego is situated in the mind and is centred on self. The higher self is situated above your head in direct line with your chakras and is therefore in direct contact with Source, the Creator of All That Is.

Many people on Earth are now questioning their existence on Earth and are wondering what their higher purpose for being here is. For many, this is a time for 'clearing out the closet' of past turmoil, negative emotions and trauma so that their higher purpose can be revealed and activated. Their souls are calling them to their life's purposes and many are answering the call. When you step into your higher purpose, which is the primary reason you incarnated, your soul will lead you because it knows where you have come from and where you have always intended to go. It is your Highest Truth. In this energy, you can feel fulfilled and peacefully happy, even if you are serving others and working hard.

In this time after Ascension, the masters, in oneness with the Creator, encourage you to get in touch with your higher self to access the knowledge that has remained dormant for so long. It is this very knowledge that can save the world from corruption, greed, war, violence and death, because, when you access this knowledge, your will raise your vibrations and begin stepping onto your spiritual path, leading you to recognise your higher purpose. Those who accept and respond to the calling of their soul to release the baggage of the past are now bringing in their lightbodies and moving into higher dimensions of light frequencies. This, dear friends, is the way to salvation because, in the ascended state, there is no room for the lower vibrations of hatred, anger, violence or judgement, only love.

Search your soul to release that which no longer serves you. Talk to your higher self through your sacred heart to remember the knowledge that you have always carried with you. See everything, including yourself, with unconditional love. Acknowledge the magic of life wherever you are, and your path will open up before you, ablaze with the light of the Creator.

WE ARE the Masters of the Cosmic Council

Meditation Four
Connect to Your Higher Mind

Be seated comfortably and close your eyes. Take three, slow abdominal breaths and feel yourself relaxing. Be aware of your physical body in the chair, your feet on the floor and the sounds around you. As you breathe in for a fourth time, envision a light coming through your crown. As you breathe out, send the light straight down through your body and deep into the Earth. Breathe in and out slowly and deeply three or four more times. With every outbreath, feel your energy going deeper, anchoring you into the Earth. Then, when you feel heavy and grounded, bring your energy and awareness back up through your body until your focus is centred in your heartspace.

Envision a beautiful, golden ball of light above your head. This is your higher, Christed self. It is the link to the wisdom you hold from all of your lifetimes and your bridge to Divine light and love. Focusing on the golden sphere of light, invite or simply bring it through your crown and down into your heartspace. As it settles into your heart area, ask that you are sitting within your higher mind and see, feel or imagine the golden light surrounding you.

Continuing to breathe in and out on an even count of four, visualise a problem, situation or person that is troubling you and ask that you be given the answer in the highest and best way for all concerned. To ensure you avoid thinking with your mind, place your hand on your heart space and focus your attention on feeling and seeing the golden energy. Allow yourself to know the answer as a thought, vision or feeling. Do not THINK, just KNOW.

When you have finished, see, feel or imagine the golden light shrinking and going back to its place above your crown. Ground your energy back into Mother Earth and bring it back to centre in your heartspace. Give thanks and gratitude to your higher mind for connecting with you and assisting you with this request.

Open your eyes when you are ready.

WE ARE yours in oneness and unconditional love,

Lord Sanada and Lady Nada

Chapter 5
Unlocking the Codes of Creation

At a crossroads in my career, I was shown a 'wall' of random, lopsided shapes and writing which I could not decipher. It was written in the blue colour of Archangel (AA) Michael who is always with me. I went to the Golden Temple with the masters of light and this is what I was told.
Blessings, Victoria

"The secrets of the Universe are not in the Universe, but in the consciousness of man and every living being on the planet. You have been shown a formula that changes and grows through integration of thought patterns and energies towards spiritual evolvement of the masses. The formula is not finite, nor is it as random as it appears. It contains specific shapes and codes to inform the mind of how to change from 3D to 5D consciousness. This is what you need to do today.

The colour blue is for the wealth of knowledge that you already have within you. The irregular shapes represent the flexibility of mind and heart, allowing changes to occur within the paradigms of thought-structures your mind accesses now. The codes are unreadable only because you are trying to 'read' them! Take your mind away and focus on one code at a time. As you see, all codes are made up of the same matter which recedes into light and become one. The codes represent creation, which cannot be read or deciphered as creation just is. The matter is moving fast just as thought patterns do: the speed at which one creates is the speed of a thought. Light thoughts manifest light opportunities just as dark, negative thoughts reap dark and negative actions and reactions. The random patterns before you represent how random thoughts become form and can create havoc and unrest in the consciousness of man. Awareness of how one's thoughts instantly create form will allow humans to regain their power of manifestation. That is what you are asked to do today.

You must work diligently to think positively and strive to see the workings of the Universe that are bringing about what you have truly desired, no matter if it does not seem so. See endings as blessings, no matter how 'messy' and uncomfortable they may be, as new beginnings give rise to new opportunities outside of your existing realities. Belief in oneself as a co-creator and powerful manifestor will immediately lift the veil of illusion to allow the Universe to assist you in your requests.

Universal Law decrees that limitations on abundance are only those created by conscious thought. When those limitations are realised and released, the realities associated with them will change; change your thoughts and perceptions and you will change your reality. Manifestation is a right, not a privilege, but with it comes serious consequences for those who manifest at the expense of the free will of another. Always ask for the Universe to give you what you need or want in the highest and best way with divine ease and grace. The intention behind the request is always the most powerful tool of the manifestation itself.

In the energy of oneness there is no need to live in poverty, scarcity or sacrifice. All in the universe is one and given to all, not just to a chosen few or to those who subscribe to certain traditions or beliefs. Now is the time to take back your power and to manifest what you want and need in your life without restrictions.

And so it is.

I AM Archangel Michael

Chapter 5

Meditation Five
Create a Positive Belief System Around Abundance

Take a few relaxing breaths and ground your energy into Mother Earth. At the same time, hold the intention that you are in the unconditional love of the Creator and surrounded by his light.

Feel yourself firmly in the present and aware of your surroundings as you hold the intention to see, feel or know the codes of creation that represent your belief system around abundance. Clear your mind and be patient as the codes are shown or revealed to you – as an image, a thought, a colour, a feeling or flash of light. Take note of how they look or feel; how positive or negative are they? How light or dark are their colours? How random or uniform are their structures?

Stand now with your feet apart and say, "I am a powerful co-creator with the abundance of the Universe at my fingertips." If your body falls backwards, you do not believe it. If it does not move, you may believe it but not know how it feels to be a powerful creator of abundance.

Give permission now for any coded information that contains limiting beliefs around your ability to manifest good things in your life, your right to be wealthy and abundant, or yourself as a powerful co-creator to now be resolved, released and transmuted to positive belief systems, along with how it feels to believe them in the highest and best way. Also hold the intention that any trauma that is held within your soul memory around lack, poverty and suffering be released from your cells and energy fields in every time, place and dimension with Divine ease and grace. Hold the energy as this happens, seeing or feeling the energy change and shift within your being. See or feel as the structures become more uniform and lighter; depending on your belief system they may even become a column of light.

Hold the intention now that the healing be grounded and integrated into your being for your highest and best.

When you feel the healing is done, stand and say again, "I am a powerful co-creator with the abundance of the Universe at my fingertips." Your body should now move forward with ease.

It is now time to create your wealth box!

Close your eyes and take three breaths to centre your energy at your crown. See, feel or imagine a beautiful, white/golden light coming down around you until you are completely surrounded by it. This is the unconditional love of the Creator and your complete protection. Now see, feel or imagine a beautiful golden box in front of you – it is like a chest. When you open the lid it is empty, ready for you to create whatever you want for the future by being grateful for what you already have in your life.

First of all, in your mind's eye, picture your family and loved ones. Give thanks for the love they give you and for the love you share together. Breathe in and then, breathing the white/golden light around them, place them lovingly in your wealth box.

Next, picture yourself. Name in your mind all of the attributes, values and personality traits that you or other people would say make the beautiful person that you are. Give thanks for the parts of your life that are happy, healthy and in balance. Breathe light and love around yourself and place yourself in the wealth box.

Now think of the job or role that you play in life and of how it positively impacts your and other people's lives. Give thanks for the money that it brings in for you (no matter how little) and for the opportunities you have been given. Breathe light and love around it all and place it all in the wealth box.

Give thanks now for any other people, things or situations you can find gratitude for and place them in the wealth box.

Now it is time to manifest what you would like to have or that you need in your life. Picture whatever it is in your mind's eye and give gratitude for it coming into your life (as if it has already happened) in the highest and best way and in the best timing for you. Breathe love and golden light around it and place it in your wealth box. Do this for everything you would like to manifest.

Remember, having gratitude for everything you already have, no matter how small or insignificant it may seem, is the key to manifesting greater wealth, health, time, happiness and love into your life.

When you have finished, close the lid on your wealth box and surround it in golden light. Give thanks and gratitude for the gifts of the Universe and then release the box into the light.

Take a moment to fill your body with the beautiful, unconditional love of the Creator before grounding your energy down through your body and opening your eyes.

I AM Archangel Metatron

Chapter 6
Unlocking Your Inner Wisdom

All humans are born with an inner knowing that transcends knowledge that has been learnt in schools or through societal teachings. This is partly because most souls living in a human body have lived hundreds or even thousands of lifetimes, but mostly because all humans on Earth are connected through Source, or 'God' as you call Him/Her, so His/Her wisdom is also their wisdom.

Those who have had a 'near-death' experience report being inexplicably drawn to a light. They also tell of the most peaceful and loving feeling they have ever experienced, with many even saying they felt like they were going home. That, my loves, is because they were! Your soul is a spoke in the Divine wheel and your spirit knows only love in the ethereal state, for the love of God the Creator is unconditional and all encompassing. He/She is the light within you that shines out to the world and that can heal in an instant, should you believe it. It also gives you access to your inner knowing.

Universal wisdom is known and remembered, not taught, although many humans awakening to their spiritual being-ness are only just becoming aware of this, even though it has always been present. If you have intuition that is never wrong, say things that are profoundly wise without prior knowledge, understand spiritual law instinctively or see/feel/know things that no-one else can, you are accessing your inner wisdom. Some people call it psychic-ness and pay to see those who show this ability but, in truth, all souls walking the Earth possess psychic abilities and Universal knowledge – they just need to learn to access it.

Not everyone possesses the same abilities and this is as it should be. The gifts you possess will very much depend upon the lives you have lived before, the lessons your soul has chosen to learn and whether you are approaching, or have achieved, mastery. The strength of your gifts will also depend on your belief in them and how much you practice – the more you use your gifts the stronger they will become and the more they will develop. In fact, many people find their gifts change over time as they become more adept, confident and trusting in them.

Allow me to list a few guiding tips to unlocking your own inner wisdom and psychic gifts:

Believe! You came from the light and are always connected to it. This connection gives you access to higher truths and spiritual wisdom.

Trust in your intuition and the guidance you are receiving. If you are strongly drawn to do something or to go somewhere, follow your instincts.

Meditate regularly. Use your breath to still your mind and to reconnect with yourself. Sit in quiet contemplation and ask your guides to connect with you.

Know who you are talking to. Learn who your guides are and always call them by name. It is a big, wide spirit world out there and you could find yourself misguided or even invaded if you are not aware of your connections.

Think with your heart, not your mind! Overthinking will only muddle you. Learn to 'know' rather than to 'think' the answer.

Read widely. There are many people who have trodden the path you find yourself on, so there are many books that may help you.

Learn to protect and control your energy. Everything in the Universe works on a trade or exchange of energy. Learn to protect your aura and, if you are empathic, avoid situations where your energy could be compromised.

Chapter 6

Release past trauma and learn to live in the moment. The past should not be there to haunt you. Learn the lessons and release the rest, or you will find yourself unable to move forward and live your full potential.

Control your thoughts. What reality are you creating for yourself? A positive mindset will create a positive reality in which only love and abundance abounds. Be grateful for what you have now, think of the positives and believe in the impossible.

See yourself and others with love and tolerance, not judgement and condemnation. Projecting lower emotions such as hatred, bitterness, anger and judgement will only block any psychic ability and spiritual connection you have.

Connect with other like-minded people who can support your journey.

Let go of ego. Being psychically connected does not make anyone more important or wiser than anyone else. Being in ego will attract lower energies that will distract you from serving and helping others and the information you receive will be much less reliable.

Learn from others. Participate in workshops, do a course or learn a new modality.

Be patient! Your gifts have always been there, but unlocking them takes time, belief and trust.

Psychic intuition and knowing is a birthright and not for the gifted few. There are many dimensions to the spiritual world and plunging into unknown territory without guidance is not recommended. If you are awakening to gifts you have been previously unaware of we, the Masters of Light, urge you to find a spiritual mentor or teacher to guide and protect you as you explore your gifts and the possibilities they offer. We also urge you to not be afraid, as fear will only block you and lower, rather than raise, your vibrations.

All humans will, at some point, be shown their psychic potential and their spiritual ancestry by their guides. Those who fully awaken and become wayshowers to others will usually have agreed to do so with their soul family before reincarnating, so their resistance or surprise level will be low. Some, however, will awaken and be frightened or overwhelmed, needing the support and guidance of people who know what is happening to them and who can guide them through it. There is never any mandate to step into one's psychic gifts; there will be no judgement from the Creator as everyone is born with free will. However, those who do will be fulfilling their soul agreements to help others to awaken and to serve humanity to the best of their ability, while also living their own lives and lessons out as planned. There is no greater gift than that!

WE ARE The Masters of the Cosmic Council

Chapter 6

Meditation Six
Connect to Your Psychic Gifts

Take a few breaths in and out, relaxing your shoulders and body as you do so. Feel yourself present in the space. Hold the intention of calling in Lord Melchizedek to assist you in connecting to your own psychic abilities for your highest and best and in the highest and best way, then hold your hands out, cupped together in front of you.

See, feel or imagine Lord Melchizedek placing a ball of light in your hands. It is a moving, vibrating ball of energy and its colour is particular to you. Focus on the light and feel the energy in your hands. How does it feel vibrationally?

Does it grow or shrink as you move your hands in and out? Try it a few times, slowly and intentionally moving your hands away from and then closer to each other. Can you feel the energy?

Now focus on seeing the colour of the light. See, feel or imagine the colour or colours of the light in your hands. What colour is it? How does it feel and what emotion does it give you?

Now imagine immersing yourself in the light. If you can 'sit' yourself in the middle of the light in your mind's eye, do so, otherwise ask me or Lord Melchizedek to surround you in the light so you can feel into its energy. How does the light make you feel? What does the colour of the light mean? If you have trouble ascertaining this, ask yourself these questions below and know, rather than think, the answer. You may even like to draw or write as you go. Always accept the first answer that comes without thought or question; you can analyse it all later!

If the colour were a word, what would it be?

If there was a place associated with the colour, where would it be?

What is the emotion attached to the colour?

What is the message of this light? Empty your mind and let it come. If necessary, write it all down.

There is a gift from Lord Melchizedek within your ball of light. Place your hands on your heartspace and allow the light to be absorbed into your being. See, feel or know what the gift in the light is – it will be conceptual and of assistance with your spiritual journey; for example, the gift of courage, self-love or a new level of confidence. Do not worry if it is not apparent at this stage, rather ask that you be shown in the way you can understand at this time. Again, focus on the gift that Lord Melchizedek has given you. Place your hands on your heartspace and allow the light to be absorbed into your being. Give yourself time to see, feel, hear or know what the gift is.

Thank Lord Melchizedek for his gift and sit quietly in the light. Reflect on how you have received the psychic messages today: were you able to see with your third eye (clairvoyance)? Did you feel or know what was happening (clairsentience)? Did you receive thoughts that were not your own as words, fragments of sentences or full messages (clairaudience)? Did you know and receive the messages quickly (claircognizance)? The strongest clair is your best way of connecting to your psychic abilities at this time. Ask me or Lord Melchizedek to guide and help you to consolidate and strengthen your abilities each time you practice.

When you are ready, recentre your energy in your heartspace and bring your attention back to the room. I advise you to keep a journal of your experiences to document your progress!

I Am AA Michael.

Chapter 7
Karmic and Soul Family Contracts

Life is fleeting, although it may last for decades or even a century which is, in human terms, a long time. Some people live long lives, while others are only on Earth very briefly. No matter how long one lives, the impact a person's life has upon the planet and the people around them is of great importance to the imprint on one's soul and the level of emotional issues it leaves.

All humans are on a soul journey from lifetime to lifetime; Earth is the 'stage' where souls act out their lessons towards evolvement and enlightenment. Many have lived countless lives and have left a large soul imprint within the fabric of consciousness that is woven between dimensions of time and space. Others have chosen to live less lifetimes in a human body but to learn larger lessons whilst in human form; so if your life is particularly hard, harsh, torturous, lonely or one of great disadvantage, it may well be that you have chosen it to be that way. One's life could be further complicated by the lessons one has chosen to learn, the trauma their soul is carrying from this or previous lifetimes or the complexities of their spirit due to upbringing, trauma or other external forces. If one leaves their current lifetime having learnt these lessons, sometimes using them to help others, the evolution of the soul towards mastery will be expedited. However, the achievement of mastery of the soul is dependent on that soul realising and acknowledging their oneness with Source on every belief level, in every soul aspect and every level of consciousness.

It may seem that the events occurring through one's life are random and unplanned, when in fact most people on Earth are living out lives that have been planned and mapped out from the time of their birth until their death: their parents, their siblings, their major lessons and higher purpose for being on Earth are all planned before birth. One's soul family will also promise to enter one's life at certain points in a lifetime in order to help keep one on track or to help in times of need or crisis. A lifetime of woe, then, is usually chosen and can be the source of major learning and fast-tracking of soul growth for that person, even though the person may not be consciously aware of it.

Another way a soul's life contract can be interrupted is through karmic intervention. Karma involves the learning of lessons, but when a lesson is learnt at the loss of will and freedom to choose without a soul-family contract, the consequences are dire and lock the soul into the wheel of karma for as long as it takes to free themselves from the debt. Many tragedies that play out on Earth, then, are actually either souls choosing to leave of their own free will, souls playing out karma or souls leaving early as a result of karmic intervention from another.

The need to play out past-life karma stems from karmic intervention from another soul or as a result of karma one has created. If one has accumulated karma from a past life, they will meet with the soul or souls involved in between carnations and plan how that karma will be replayed in the next lifetime. So, if a soul has been responsible for a single death, then the victim will instigate or facilitate a repayment of the contract in the next lifetime. However, if the soul has been responsible for a multitude of deaths, such as a holocaust or a bombing that takes many innocent lives, the consequences will be far more serious and lengthy in terms of the number of reincarnations needed to repay the karmic debt. A soul who has lost their way in such a devastating way can spend thousands of extra lifetimes repaying every soul that was lost at their will.

The human spirit is not human although, when grounded in a physical, human body, it takes on a personality of its own, attaches to ego and can sometimes become disconnected from its divine blueprint. The spirit travels within the soul and can reincarnate over hundreds or even thousands of human lifetimes. Although the soul remains the same throughout its many reincarnations, it fractures each time, leaving a bit of itself in the memory of the last lifetime. The spirit, or essence of personality, changes each time according to past experiences, the amount of trauma the soul is still carrying and the lessons it has chosen to learn this lifetime. An incarnated soul can carry more than one memory of lifetimes, called aspects, which influence the personality and belief systems of the incarnated soul. Sometimes one aspect can be dominant. It may also take on the role of the Higher, Christed Self, which is the bridge from the human mind to divine understanding. This is more the case with highly evolved souls.

The spirit lives on after physical death and reconnects to the light of Source, which is the *All* and encompasses all of Creation. As the energy of Source is unconditional, no spiritual being knows or recognises separation from the All or any of the emotions that humans feel. This fact can make reincarnation into a human body in the dense energy of third dimensional Earth particularly difficult for older or highly evolved souls; to exist in a world that is often harsh, disconnected and conflicted goes against every instinct of the spirit, which knows only oneness and boundless love.

The spirit is not bound to reincarnate just on Earth and many spirits carried within souls in human form at this time have experienced life on other planets and/or as intelligence without a form at all. The knowledge of the soul, however, is far less accessible when weighed down by the human mind, which concerns itself with matters of the self, materialism, emotional feelings and illusions of religion, stature and wealth. Lifetimes of loneliness, disconnection and sustained hardship can affect the spirit residing within the soul, causing the build-up of negative emotions, disconnection, grief and trauma.

Those who have experienced violent or tragic deaths in previous lifetimes can be especially affected and, if not released, traumatic and negative memories can remain with the soul across many lifetimes, keeping the spirit trapped in cycles of learning that are detrimental to their spiritual growth and evolvement. Worse still, the spirit can become disconnected from the soul which houses it, causing the incarnated human to become disconnected from Source and their spiritual self, trapped within their physical body and completely overwhelmed by third dimensional energies. This is a devastation from which many souls cannot recover, resulting in some of them ending their incarnation before their soul contract is complete.

Suicide, which is a common decision of disconnected souls, can result in the fracturing of spirit from the soul which takes much longer to heal between lifetimes. It can also result in the soul reincarnating too quickly to make amends, only to find themselves in much the same position as before. There is no judgement from the ethereal kingdom and the Creator for souls ending their contracts early, for this action can be seen as a valuable lesson in itself. However, suicide does transgress the spiritual law of harmlessness, causing ramifications in terms of spiritual law. Leaving one's lifetime early usually means that the soul has not had a chance to resolve all of their karma and/or to learn all of their lessons, interrupting their journey to mastery, so they will need to reincarnate again to do so.

There is no judgment from God, the Supreme Creator, if a soul has lost their way and killed or harmed themselves, others or the planet. The judgment comes from their fellow humans throughout their lifetime and the soul itself, whose life review after death will determine the next course of action it needs to take; either to be reborn to continue to repay karmic death, or to stay in spirit to learn amongst one's soul family for a longer time before coming back. Those souls who are close to or have already achieved mastery may choose to be reborn again to remain in service and assist humans on Earth to evolve and grow, and their soul aspects can be embedded in many human forms at the same time. The wisdom these souls bring is active on Earth now and many of you may know them as your teacher, advisor, mentor, friend or family member.

If you currently find yourself going though events that are hard to deal with, or if your life is constantly hard or in turmoil, consider this: what have you learnt and what are the blessings you can use to build upon? How are your thoughts attracting or not attracting better things into your life and how can you, as the only one who can take one hundred percent responsibility for your life, turn things around for the better? No matter whether it is because you have made 'bad' choices or the tide has turned against you, there is always an opportunity to use adversity as a gateway for learning, evolvement and new beginnings; a glass half full is always better than one half empty, even if one needs to work at believing it.

Humans are not the only 'animals' to carry their spirit in a living, functioning body. On Earth, any warm-blooded mammal has a spirit carried within a soul that can reincarnate again and again. The difference between human souls and other mammals is that they can learn to love and be loved conditionally and to see themselves as separate from Source, whereas all other mammals retain their connection to the oneness and unconditional love of the Creator throughout their lifetimes. Is it possible, then, for the human spirit to reincarnate as another mammal, such as a dog or a cat? It is possible, but it is very rare. This is because the souls of mammals other than humans have already reached mastery; they never waiver from their connection to the unconditional love of Source and to them, everything just is. In the natural world, all animals live in symbiosis with the natural world and for the greater good of all. They rely on their instinct, ancestral and genetic knowledge to live, but can adapt to change if the need arises. Humans also have instinctual, ancestral and genetic knowledge within their DNA, but they find it much more difficult to adapt to their surroundings without using outside resources, such as clothing, heating etc.

So, does genetic information of how to be a particular species of mammal only reside in the physical body? Even though different species of mammals have particular characteristics and behave in much the same way, anyone who has owned a cat, dog, pig, horse or any other mammal will tell you they had their own personalities. This is the same with humans. Why is it, then, that mammals know how to live and behave in a certain way and that individuals of a particular species look the same while developing their own unique personalities?

The genetic makeup of every type of animal is like a shell waiting to be filled. While the DNA of every species of mammal is passed on from parents to child, bringing the form to life, the soul fills the physical vessel with the spirit that gives the body its personality and will to carry out their personal mission on Earth. If the spirit leaves the soul before the physical body has died, the human will only exist as a vegetable would, without any spark of the person who lived before.

Many of the aspirations a person may have in life will not be relevant after they die; what seems important now will have no consequence at all in one's ethereal form. The Earthly Plane is an illusion that tricks the soul into believing that everything that happens in life is real and that material possessions, status and wealth are important, healthy and normal goals. Consider, for one moment, the person who has none of the above things, yet who is extremely happy with his or her life. Why or how is this so? They have no money, no fancy car or big house, but they are comfortable with who they are. How can they be so happy when they have so little? The answer has to do with one's God-self, the part of every individual that is eternally connected to Source and that knows oneness with the Creator and the All. Owning the most expensive possessions does not ensure happiness, nor does it mean they make an honourable or even a likeable person. The integrity one's soul possesses will be evident whether they are the richest person in the world or the poorest! No amount of wealth and the trappings it provides can hide the integrity of one's soul or any ego behind a person's behaviour.

Think for a moment: after you have passed over and have looked back on your life, what will you see? Will you see a person who did their best to honour their own integrity, to speak their truth and to live an honest life, or will you see someone whose aim it was to show how important they were through the possessions they owned and through the lies they spoke? There is no hiding from the Creator, who knows the integrity of your soul and who loves you unconditionally no matter how rich or poor you may be. Are you being honest with yourself about your happiness? Are you truly happy and content within yourself, or is everything you own and do in life a smoke screen to cover what you may consider to be the blemishes and faults within yourself? Strip it all back, Dear Ones, and find what is truly important within you. When you are honest with yourself and begin to speak and stand in your truth, the faults that you see now will suddenly seem like true blessings, ones that have the potential to bring you into a state of oneness and peace with the Creator and the All.

It is the only way forward.

I AM Archangel Metatron

Chapter 7

Meditation Seven
Clear the Soul of Past Life Trauma and Resolve Karmic Debt

Take three breaths and centre yourself in your heart and soul space. Call upon me, Archangel Metatron, to surround you in my silver light and to connect you to the unconditional love of the Universe. Continue breathing in and out, working on slowing your breath and relaxing your body. When you are ready, focus all of your attention on your soul space and repeat this command:

"I now hold the intention of integrating all of the lessons of my past lifetimes and of resolving, releasing and healing all related karmic ties and debts, associated trauma, psychic hooks and attachments and links to all persons past and present that no longer serve my greatest good. Send it all to the light of Source and heal my bodies, cells, organs and energy fields until they are free of all of this discordant energy. Do this with Divine ease, grace and intelligence, to be witnessed by Archangel Metatron until it is done. So it is."

Continue focusing your attention on your breathing and willingly open your heart and soul space to the release. If you feel a resistance, ask me to bring in the Violet Flame of Transmutation to clear blockages of resentment, anger, lack of forgiveness and bitterness. See, feel, visualise or imagine the energy change and your body becoming lighter, freer and more relaxed.

When you feel or know it is done, give thanks and gratitude to the Universe for the healing and for your continuing happiness, health and abundance. Fill your heart and soul space with love and gratitude then release it out to the Universe with your breath. Then, breathing in, ground your energy and feel my loving blessing.

I AM Archangel Metatron

Chapter 8
The Spirit of God

The human body is flesh and bone, but the human spirit is the essence of the Source of Creation. It is one with God's light and there is no separation between them. When one's body dies, the spirit returns to the light and becomes part of that light as if it had never left. In life, if one loses connection to or belief in the light, the possibility of returning to the light in death is never diminished; it will still occur just as certainly as night follows day.

The fallacies believed by the human mind mean that disconnection from God and the His/Her love becomes almost as certain as one's return to it upon death. The illusions of the physical world can block the subconscious mind's ability to remain faithful and connected, meaning that the person begins to believe a raft of un-truths about their spirituality and infinite connection to Source as a ray of God's light. The travesty of injustices upon human lives on Earth cannot be undone or released from the human spirit unless one consciously intends to do so. Being aware of one's infinite connection to Source will expedite the process; in the energy of the Creator instant healings and manifestation are a right of all beings on Earth, not a privilege of a chosen few. Those who have such knowledge, or seek the assistance of someone who does, are now lifting the ties that bind them to past events and lives on Earth that have left enormous traumatic imprints on their soul memories, which in turn have caused damage to their spiritual connection and beliefs. The more that people can release emotional baggage and return to the love and light of the Creator as a rite of passage through self-belief and empowerment, the more they will be much less likely to continue to allow the illusions of drama on Earth to entrap their spirit and soul in darkness and despair.

There is no hope if one cannot believe it to be so. The amount of negativity generated by people across the globe who are buying into fear is bringing the world to its knees. It is a challenge to those who are working feverishly with the Creator and their guides to stay above the drama and to raise the vibrations of the world around them to the Fifth Dimension. If one's soul carries the scars of the past, it is much more difficult to believe in love or that there is a God at all. The power to maintain belief and connection rests upon one's ability to shrug off the ghosts of the past and to see the Earth and its inhabitants as the Creator does: as perfect in every way. Each living being is a unique individual and loved unconditionally, despite any laws that they have broken, the number of mistakes they have made or any beliefs they do or don't hold.

The love of the Creator is in every object, living thing and being in the Universe and the joy of Creation is the foundation upon which the spirit thrives. If one cannot feel that they are a co-creator and thus in charge of their own lives and realities, they have lost their power and ability to forge change. A broken or downtrodden spirit will not be able to find the light of Creation inside of themselves and will consequently look outside of themselves for fulfilment. This can become a never-ending cycle of self-sabotage as, unable to give themselves the love that their spirit craves (as the love given to oneself is also the love of the Creator), they become desperate to fill the void through drugs, alcohol, crime, narcissism and even violence. These people will never be happy and will, in turn, create unhappiness in the lives of others, unless they can address the issues that are weighing them down and that have damaged their spiritual connection.

The journey of life continues through death and through incarnation after incarnation. Each lifetime brings a new physical body and a new set of experiences to navigate through, but the spiritual essence remains the same, just as that of the Creator. The memories of each lifetime help to shape the lifetime that is being currently lived, and the shape of one's experiences will depend on the amount of trauma one has managed to release or that is still being carried within the soul.

The message to remember, Dear Ones, is that, through life and beyond it, your connection to the Creator will never be lost. You are never separate and never alone. In finding connection, many look to religion and that is as it may be. However, connection to the light and love of Creation is within every rock, plant, insect, animal and being, human or otherwise, in the Universe. There is no attachment to any religion or boundary required, as the love and light of the Creator is within every creation, unconditionally and completely.

Look no further for God than within yourself, Dear Hearts. You are a spoke of the Divine wheel and the light and love of God is within you. Connect to yourself and go within. When you can do feel His/Her love, His/Her light will shine out to the world, because unconditional love is of the highest order and the nectar of the human spirit.

I Am Lord Melchizedek.

Meditation Eight
Connect to the Unconditional Love of Source

Breathe deeply and relax your body and mind with each outbreath. See, feel or imagine a light coming through your crown, connecting you to the Divine light and love of the Source of Creation. Feel the strength of the energy as it descends through your body, connecting your chakras as it goes down deep into Mother Earth.

Now bring your focus back to your crown chakra and see, feel, visualise or imagine its violet colour as it slowly surrounds you, until you find yourself sitting on top of it and within it. It looks and feels like a lotus flower with infinite petals. If you cannot see or feel it, know that with focused intention it still is. Continue breathing steadily in a relaxed manner, drawing the beautiful energy of the crown chakra into your being. If you find your head is filled with a lot of pressure, ask that the energy be matched to your vibration in the highest and best way and that any lower vibrations be transmuted and cleansed by the violet light.

Feel yourself rising now into the white, sparkling light of the Creator. As you do so, your lotus flower turns to white; you are now one with the unconditional love of Source. In this energy there are no people or things; everything just is. As you feel yourself merging with and becoming one with the light, allow yourself to trust and to just be. Allow the feeling of love to wash through you, cleansing negativity, pain, anxiety and fear and returning your body to balance.

When you are ready, slowly and steadily bring your focus

back to the violet light of the crown chakra. Send the violet light down through your body to ground into Mother Earth and then to centre in your heart space. You feel peaceful and very loved.

It is possible to remain in this energy for the rest of the day. Simply give thanks for your continued connection and protection, bring your awareness back into your body and continue with your day.

I AM the Creator of All That Is

Chapter 9
The Human Collective Consciousness

In the energy of the Creator of All That Is, everything and everyone in the Universe is One. There is no separation from the Source of Creation, even though many people on the Earth believe or feel it to be so. The connection between humans is therefore intrinsic and infinite, with every thought, word, feeling and intention emitted by every human alive on the planet collecting around the globe as a mass of fluctuation and ever-changing energy. It is called the Human Collective Consciousness and it affects everyone in different and varying ways.

This 'cloud' of energy is a complete mish-mash of feelings and emotions ranging from hatred to love, despair to joy, loss and emptiness to overwhelming happiness. As the emotions of every individual change throughout the day, so does the amount of negativity or positivity in the consciousness. The location of where a particular thought or emotion was emitted makes no difference, because the energy mixes with existing energy, fluctuating, changing and travelling around the Earth at any given time. In places where extreme events are occurring, such as war, natural disaster or travesties against humanity, pockets of deep negativity may remain for some time. This is why it is so important for every human to be careful of the vibration of their thoughts and to send love to the world whenever they can.

People can be affected by the human collective consciousness without being aware of it and this is where the danger lies. Waves of love and positivity will not do any harm if they come over a person unexpectedly but, when hit by a sudden wave of inexplicable anger and unexplained hatred that originally emanated from a person or group with extremist views, unwitting and innocent people can suddenly become violent without explanation. Those whose vibrations are already low due to substance abuse, poverty, extreme hunger or hardship are particularly vulnerable, because low vibrations will attract more of the same. Empathic people, or those who are sensitive to the energy around them, are also at risk. As the plight of humanity deepens and the grips of corruption and manipulation tighten, this is a timely reminder to all to protect your energy and remain vigilant.

It is not our intention to discuss the darker forces who have been at play in the world. Rather, it is much more critical to stress the importance of spiritual connection to the unconditional love of the Creator. When one operates from the love of Source, lower energies cannot penetrate the aura or soul of the person. It is critical for each and every person on the Earth to extricate themselves from the illusion of the drama and materialism of the Earthly plane and to connect to their own divinity. Meditate, pray for assistance and begin to see the world through the lens of love, gratitude and service. Be conscious of your thoughts and feelings, because they create your reality and add to the consciousness of the masses. Work towards becoming a master of your own destiny and take responsibility for your thoughts, words, actions and reactions to others. Only you can change your world for the better. It starts with mindfulness and ends with mastery. Ask me to guide you.

I AM Archangel Michael

Chapter 9

Meditation Nine
Heal Your Bodies and Energy Fields

Breathe deeply and center your energy, first in your heartspace, then breathe it down to your abdomen. Feel it extending right down into Mother Earth and up to Creator's light as you do so. Acknowledge your connection with the All. Breathe deeply from your abdomen, filling your lungs to the top, then releasing the air until it is all expelled. Repeat this three times. Be sure to expand your abdomen outwards as you breathe in as well. If you need to do it a few more times to relax, do so.

Now, feeling your feet on the floor and your body sitting in the chair, release all concept of time and space. Feel yourself floating upwards, as if out of your body, all the time knowing you are safely grounded. Feel your body melting into space, becoming one with the air and its molecules. Let go completely, allowing your physical body to meld with your spiritual body and its surroundings. In this state there is no pain, no fear and no emotional trauma. You just are -part of the All and completely one with it.

Now, as you are suspended in time and space, see, feel or imagine the light of Archangel Raphael. The green, healing light completely surrounds and protects you as it melds with your physical and spiritual bodies, cleansing each molecule, each cell and every part of you. Feel his love as it completely wipes away painful memories and brings you to a total state of peace, wellbeing and gratitude. As you are engulfed in his healing green light, you see the light turn bright white, then golden. Breathe in and out gently on a count of four as your bodies are all merged with light, cleansing, purifying and healing you.

Now envision a beautiful, white lotus flower in your heart space. As you focus on it, see, feel or imagine it growing larger as it begins floating up towards your crown. As it settles on the top of your crown, watch as the stem of the lotus flower grows down through your chakra line, connecting all of your chakras down to your Earth chakra, anchoring your energy deep down into Mother Earth. See, feel or imagine roots growing out of the stem, firmly anchoring you into the Earth. The leaves are your chakras, which all begin to spin as you bring your energy slowly back up again, cleansing, balancing, aligning and activating each one to its highest frequency.

As you again reach your crown, you find yourself sitting in the lotus position on top of your white lotus flower, which now has 1000 petals. Regulating your breathing to four breaths in and four breaths out, you feel peaceful and calm as the pure energy of the lotus flower permeates your being. See, feel or know you are a being of light sitting upon the white lotus flower, gradually becoming one with it, until there is no separation. You feel absolutely pure of mind, body, heart and spirit and totally at one, not only with the lotus but with the Creator and the Universe. In this space everything just is... you just ARE. Continue focusing on the pure, bright white light and your breath as you send love to yourself, your family and the world.

When you are ready, consciously bring your energy back until you can see or feel yourself sitting back on the lotus flower. Bring your energy back up from the Earth to your crown, then bring yourself back down and centre in your heart space. You feel grounded, peaceful and totally relaxed.

Gently and gradually, bring yourself back to the chair. Feel your feet on the ground and your breath in your lungs. Bring your energy back up from your abdomen, center it in your heartspace and take a moment to allow the healing to integrate into your being.

We Are Archangel Raphael and Quan Yin

Part 2

The Gift of Life on Earth: Connecting to the Elements of Nature

Chapter 10
The Love of Mother Earth

If the whole world could see the light coming from within Mother Earth, they would be amazed! Yes, on a physical level the middle of the Earth is fiery, hot and molten, but on a spiritual, ethereal level it holds a crystalline diamond core. It is a heart that beats as your heart beats, feels as your heart feels and breaks as a heart can break. Mother Earth feels every human emotion and she reflects it all back to the planet as vibrational energy. This energy then becomes a part of the way of life on Earth, including changes in the weather patterns, sudden and catastrophic natural disasters, a holding of spirit energy in places where dark actions against others have occurred; even in the way humans interact with each other on a daily basis. However, the love of Mother Earth, for all who live upon her, is a direct reflection of the love of the Creator, because all on Earth and beyond is one with the Creator and the energy of the Universe. When people give love to themselves and each other, even if they have not been previously acquainted, this love radiates out to other people and other life forms, absorbing into the Earth's heart, as well as into the Human Collective Consciousness.

Do not be deluded by all of the drama, grandstanding and bloodshed going on around the world at this time, because it is all like a magician's smoke screen. As those who wish to keep the world in darkness towards their own ends continue to rule with fear and mind control, people are awakening to the light and are coming into their power. There has been a mass awakening over the last twelve to eighteen months and the grips of darkness are loosening. Those who refuse to be swayed by propaganda are waging their own war of sorts against the darkness that is spread by lies, domination and fear. They are sending love and light to the world and the counteractive effect cannot be underestimated! Remember, with intent it is, so visualisation with intent is all that is needed to manifest change; when it is sent with intent from a group the effect is magnified even more.

Fear divides, while love unites. There is no other way to rid the Earth of hatred, fear, despair, terrorism and war than people loving one another despite any differences they may have. God does not judge, as He/She has given the Earth to humans as the stage to learn their lessons towards soul growth, mastery and enlightenment. He/She loves all of humanity and holds it in His/Her light, willing all to see that His/Her love and light is available free from religious bias and doctrine. The word of God is love, that is all.

If you are feeling affected by the doom and gloom reported on and exaggerated by the media, the best thing to do is to remove yourself from it. Do not watch the news or engage in talk around the doctrine, prophesies and, sometimes, diseases that are being spread like wildfire across the globe. The illusion of what is occurring in the world will only serve to erode your love and bring you into feelings of fear, hatred and revenge. Remember that you are all connected in the world and what you think will add fuel to the fire, that is, to the negativity in the universal consciousness. Send love to those affected and to the perpetrators. Love is the only emotion that can truly raise the world out of its third dimensional state.

Love is the reason that Mother Earth's heart is still beating, because without her connection to Source she would have lost her way in the face of the battering of negative human emotions over so many centuries. The beings of light that exist in tandem with the Earthly Plane, including the many Lightworkers who have awoken to assist Mother Earth in her quest to ascend to the Fifth Dimension, are working tirelessly through many blockages to raise the vibrational patterns of light from darkness to brilliance. Just as the sun shines, so does the heart and soul of every being who is working with Mother Earth; this light is working to bring the Earth and all who live upon her out of the denseness and darkness of ego and hatred into the brilliant light of unconditional love, peace and oneness. All every person needs to do is to love themselves and others for who they are with no judgement or conditions. It really is that simple.

Chapter 10

Although it may seem that all on Earth is in turmoil in so many ways, the energies that are now emerging are iridescent, calming and of pure essence. They emerge from Mother Earth herself as she comes into alignment with planets outside her solar system and merges her energies with theirs. The vibrations are of pure oneness and the colours are deep purples, blues, pinks, yellows and white. The power of these energies cannot be underestimated; it is now more important than ever that the fear-mongering of those who have encompassed lower energies not be allowed to permeate greater society, even though their attempts are ferocious and very frightening.

Remember, beloveds, that nothing on the Earthly plane is real. It is all an illusion as you play out your lessons and life's purposes towards mastery; the reason you incarnated was to save the Earth and to help her ascend. Love is the only vibration and emotion that is real and the only one that can save your planet. Disconnect from the drama that surrounds you and reconnect with your Higher Self, because it knows your true purpose and your soul journey and it will help you to connect with your ethereal self, your guides and the Creator Himself. The Creator's energy is that of oneness and unconditional love and it is the only energy that will allow you to view the world with no judgement. Those of you who are awakened will be aware of the emerging energies and will know how to harness and spread them to the world. It is essential that you teach others and help those around you to become aware and awake also.

The energies emanating from Mother Earth are directly connected to your sacred fire, as your connection to Mother Earth is integral to your being. When you focus your energy in your sacral chakra and connect to your sacred fire, the new energies will emanate from your heart chakra out to the world. With practise and intention, this emanation will occur whether you are conscious of it or not.

Love is all there is, Dear Ones! Everything else is an illusion and will only become reality if you believe it to be so. Do not buy into the illusion of darkness, because the duality of light and dark is not in the energy of the Creator. When you see, feel and become love you are one with God's light, nothing else is real. Believe in love, even if you cannot believe in God. See love as the only energy that is real and send it with purpose to the world; you cannot imagine how powerful that one act can be.

I AM Archangel Michael

Meditation Ten
Healing for Mother Earth

Ensure that you are sitting or lying in a comfortable position with your eyes closed. Concentrate on your breath, ensuring that when you breathe in you fill your lungs to the top, expanding your abdomen as you do. When you breathe out, expel the air slowly and gently, feeling your body relax a little more each time. Breathe in, breathe out, falling into an easy and regular rhythm, not over breathing or thinking. Your mind will wish to think, so concentrate on your breath and your body, releasing stress and tension from a different part of your body as you go, starting from your head and working down to your feet.

Now concentrating on your feet, feel or see a light growing around them. It is coming from Mother Earth, anchoring you and grounding your energy into hers. The light is clear and bright, soft and safe, and it is moving upwards to encase your entire body. As you are completely surrounded by this light, you now become aware of a brighter light coming into your crown. This is your connection to the Divine Source and will allow you to send your energy out to the world while completely protecting you. The bright, white pearlescent light moves down through your chakras, aligning, balancing and activating them to a higher vibration. It is moving down through your third eye, now your throat, your higher heart, your heart, your diaphragm, solar plexus, sacral, base and then down to your Earth Chakra. If you do not feel or see it, know it to be so.

You are now completely relaxed, grounded and connected to Mother Earth and the Creator. Continue breathing in an out and see the light that has entered your body centering in your heartspace. Feel the love within this ball of light – it is your love, merged with the love of Mother Earth and of the Creator.

Now, intend to send this love to the Earth, magnified 1000 times by angelic energy and distributed in the highest and best way, for your highest and best and for the greater good. Then, in your mind's eye, hold the intention that you see Mother Earth before you. If you cannot see, imagine it. You may see the whole Earth or just a part of it. You may feel drawn to send the love and light to animals, plants, waterways, humans or to parts of the Earth where there is suffering. We do this by the Law of Grace and without the intention of intervening on anyone's free will. We also hold the intention that our love and light be sent as a group endeavour and that it be combined with the Violet Flame of Transmutation to assist Mother Earth to shed the 3D energy that is holding her to the lower dimensions.

Your love and light is so bright you can hold it no longer. As it flies from your heartspace it is met with the Violet Flame, and the impact on the Earth is immediate. See or feel the vibrations and colours change as the healing occurs, while staying mindful of being grounded and connected, fully protected and safe as you send this healing to the world. Watch as the healing occurs and notice the changes in colours, the release of negativity which will all be sent to God's light. Hold the energy until the healing is over.

See or feel the light in your heart space growing smaller. The light from Mother Earth returns to your feet but your connection to the Creator remains. The healing you have just sent to the Earth has also helped to heal you. Focus now on the parts of your body that have received healing and allow it to integrate, releasing any feelings or emotions that arise.

When you are finished, hold the intention of breaking your energy from the meditation and bring your awareness back to the room. You feel lighter, more energised and totally relaxed.

I AM Master Kathumi.

Chapter 11
The Magic of Life

Magic is always seen by humans as a fantasy or just a slight of the hand, when in fact there is magic all around you, if only you would take the time to notice it. Magic abounds on Earth in nature as well as in the ethereal kingdom and is available to all who believe in it, appreciate it and use it for the greater good and/or in the highest and best way.

The magic of nature is not just in the song of the birds, the whisper of wind in the trees or the babble of the rippling stream. The magic is in the way life abounds on Earth and how it is reproduced to fit the environment or habitat of each lifeform in just the right way. Life itself is the magic, because it is a wonder of nature that has never found explanation. How is it that the human body, or the body of any creature on Earth, has been developed in just the right way for it to fully function as a complete system that can, in the right conditions, regenerate and heal itself completely? How is it that the different elements on Earth compliment themselves and fit together so well? How did it come about that the food sources for each species on Earth happens to be in abundance within the same ecosystem? Have you ever really wondered at how symbiotic the natural world is and how it actually came to be? That, My Dears, is the magic of nature and the magic of life.

Birth itself is a miracle that happens every second of every day and the formation and growth of the foetus into a fully grown being is a wonder to behold. Conception is the moment of creation when two beings come together as one and is a truly magical moment. Animals procreate instinctually and as part of their natural cycle, but humans, for the most part, procreate as a result of a loving relationship. The miracle of bringing a child into the world is, for many parents, the most wonderful and cherished time of their lives. For others it is an event that they would rather avoid, or that they do without considering the vast responsibilities that accompanies the arrival of a baby. The choice to continue with such a pregnancy is one that can have lifelong consequences for the parents and the soul they are bringing into the world.

The miracle and magic of life is something that must be respected and held sacred. To deliberately take a life is a travesty that is felt enormously in the ethereal kingdom, even if it is the life of an ant or a fly. All life is sacred and of the utmost importance; there is no separation between insects, animals and humans in the level of sacredness, for all is one and everything equal in the energy of the Creator of All That Is. Respect life and you will show respect to yourself and the world you have chosen to live in.

The magic of life is no more evident than in the natural world. When people have lost their zest for life they would do well to reconnect to nature and Mother Earth. When people talk about 'getting back to nature', they often go out into the bush, up into the mountains or at least many miles from home in order to do so. For many, nature is somewhere that is removed from civilisation, away from the crowds and a place that is unspoiled by human touch.

While it may be true that it is easier to 'feel' nature in these places, the fact remains that getting back to nature is as easy as walking barefoot on your back lawn and blocking out the sounds of suburbia around you. Nature is all around us, even in the city. If you cannot escape from the city, look to the sky or sit under a tree! Sit in the park at lunch time or put a plant on your desk. It is possible to connect with Mother Earth and the natural surrounds in some way even when time or work restraints do not allow it at the present time. You will be surprised at how healing doing so can be.

The reason that humans have the in-built need to connect to nature is that humans are one with nature. In the energy of the Creator, everything is one and connected. The need to connect and ground to Mother Earth comes from the fact that she is connected to every human's soul. When you connect and ground to her you will immediately feel more centred and more level-headed.

The natural world is in balance. Everything works symbiotically to create

Chapter 11

a harmonious state that just works. Connecting to nature will help you to remain grounded and more focused towards daily tasks without becoming emotionally drained or overloaded. When you tap into the frequency of complete balance and oneness which emanates from the natural world, you will begin to see and appreciate the wonder and magic of life in all its forms. Get back to nature, dear ones, and bring yourself back to balance and harmony. If everyone did this, the world would have been much closer to Ascension by now.

And so it is.

I AM Merlin

Meditation Eleven
Connect to Nature

Make sure you are hydrated. Sit comfortably and take a few breaths to centre and ground your energy.

Centre your energy in your heart space and connect to the light of Creation (God, the Creator). You can do this through prayer or clear intention. This is your protection while your consciousness is outside your body. Feel the energy surrounding and protecting you.

In your mind's eye, see a forest: you are walking down a track into a deep, green forest. You can hear the birds calling and the rustling of insects in the leaves on the forest floor. It is cool and shady and you feel calm and relaxed. You soon come to a clearing with a circular patch of grass in the centre - you reach it and sit down; it feels cool and soft. As you sit on the grass, some butterflies come to rest on your shoulders, and tiny birds peck at your feet. A rabbit comes to graze on the grass nearby and other animals appear. They will be different for each one of you, so take the time to notice what they are. There is a calmness around you as the natural world envelops you.

The trees are rustling quietly in the breeze and you feel the cool breeze on your face. Your body feels connected to the grass, which is connected to the Earth and to the unconditional love of the Source of Creation and the Universe. Feel the certainty of this love and your place in the world. Feel love for yourself as you continue on the journey of life. Breathe in the light and love of Creation.

If there is a universal language linking humans to nature, it

Chapter 11

is love. Fill you heart with love and send it to the animals, plants, earth and air around you. Feel the energy around you become warmer as you breathe in and out, breathing in light and breathing in love.

Take time now to see the beautiful garden you have created with the breath of love. See flowers of every type and colour, butterflies, birds, and bees. Notice other features that have appeared, such as any creeks, ponds, water fountains or waterfalls. This is now your special garden that you can return to at any time. Stay in this space until you feel totally relaxed and grounded, at one with your surrounds and the light of Source.

Ground back down and give thanks for your abundance and the gifts in your life. Centre yourself back in your heartspace and open your eyes. You will feel refreshed, renewed and rejuvenated.

I AM Merlin

Chapter 12
The Patterns of Life

The patterns of life are all around us in the natural world; bees and wasps have stripes, so do zebras, the pattern for each individual being original and unique. The network of veins in every single leaf forms a pattern of life; butterflies and moths have distinctive patterns according to their species, as do tigers, jaguars and cheetahs. All humans have fingerprints which, again, are unique to every individual. Yes, patterns are everywhere in the world, some being generic but many being as unique and individual as the creature itself.

Patterns are what make up the Universe, but not always in shape. Many are in colour, as in a rainbow, and others are in numeric codes. Everything in the universe can be reduced to a sequential pattern that has its own vibrational frequency, or 'DNA' if you like, that distinguishes its molecular structure from every other organism on the Earth, whether it be living or non-living. This pattern of life is a code that underwrites the look, distinguishing features and behaviour of the organism, keeps the species breeding and surviving and generally cannot be changed. However, there is a natural law of evolution that states that change in structure can and must occur in response to changes in the natural environment and, to that end, many species of organisms are undergoing molecular changes within their DNA structures in order to adapt to the ever-changing landscapes and weather patterns on Earth. Humans are one of these species undergoing evolutionary change at this time.

Sacred geometry is what underpins all codes in the Universe, whether they be of matter, light or sound. The symmetry of any geometrical structure ensures its exact reproduction time and time again. The symmetrical codes within any lifeform's DNA, such as in a species of flower, the shapes of leaves on different species of tree or of the features of different forms of insects will ensure the continuation of the species, as long as it remains undamaged.

The patterns of life upon the Earth have been radically changed by man's interventions such as the use of fossil fuels and unnatural chemicals. Many organisms, including humans, have been affected and infected by pollution and the ingestion of toxic materials that are often in food that has been consumed. The results are disease, sickness and mutations that shorten the life span of the individual and that often threaten the existence of the entire species. Changes in DNA structures throw out the original balance between the species and the environment and this then continues down the food chain. Earth has lost many of its precious plants and animals to man's predisposition to killing for entertainment and sport, but the loss of life to unnatural mutations from toxins, chemicals and diseases will have a far greater impact on life on Earth unless urgent action is taken. The death of millions of humans from diseases and cancers is testament to the physical body's inability to cope with foreign substances and food that is not in alignment with the natural world; when the pattern of life is interfered with, the consequences can be dire.

It is understood by the masters of light that humans may feel helpless at the whim of governments and leaders who make decisions based on profit rather than on humanitarian terms. Many decisions are made without consultation and often with no communication, leading to the consumption of toxins and chemicals, either through food, absorption or breathing, without peoples' direct knowledge. People may also feel helpless against corporations who use less-than-worthy ingredients in their products in order to make them more palatable, even though they are unhealthy and often carcinogenic. Many people are now turning towards natural ingredients and raw, organic food and are also rejecting western medicine, even if they are considered to be terminally ill; in many cases, the intervention towards a cure is worse than the disease itself and causes more harm than intended.

It is not the intention of this message to advise anyone against going to a doctor or of seeking medical assistance when they are ill. It IS intended, however, to convey the importance of maintaining the balance between systems in the world and of not interfering too much in the natural order of life. When

Chapter 12

balance can be sustained then the health of the organism and the environment will also be maintained. As soon as the balance is thrown out, it is not just the individual and the immediate environment that is affected. At present, much of the world's natural balance has been disrupted and this has impacted the health and well-being of all living things upon it. The patterns have been changed, and the consequences have the potential to change the world as you all know it forever.

I AM Lord Melchizedek

Meditation Twelve
Transmute Pollutants and Greenhouse Gasses

For this meditation we will be going to the Seventh Plane to ensure your energetic protection, then we will be sending energy from the Crystalline Lightworkers' Grid.

Ground your energy into Mother Earth, harnessing her love and protection with intention, then take your energy as light up through your chakras until it is a ball of energy rotating above your crown. Hold the intention of bringing the light of the Creator of All That Is down to merge with yours and see, feel or imagine His/Her beautiful pearlescent white light becoming one with yours. Taking a breath in, breathe out and bring His/Her light down around you. Take a few moments to merge your energy into the unconditional love of the Creator, feeling the bliss of all-that is, safe, protected and one.

We call now upon Archangel Metatron to transport you to the Crystalline Grid to send healing to the planet. See, feel or imagine yourself being anchored into your vortex of light on the grid, which surrounds the Earth in its glowing light. Take a moment to allow the pulsating energy of the grid to clear and heal you, then see the Earth below you and Archangel Metatron beside you, ready to assist you.

Now hold the intention of an unconditional healing for the atmosphere around the Earth to transmute dangerous greenhouse gasses to harmless. See, feel or imagine the atmosphere becoming more visible, particularly those areas that are most affected by greenhouse gasses. You may see *murky colours, holes, or you may see it as ultra-violet light energy. Use this invocation for the healing:*

"Mother, Father God, Creator of All That Is, it is intended that all greenhouse gasses, pollutants, chemicals and toxins in the atmosphere around the Earth in every time, place and dimension be transmuted to harmless using the Violet Flame of Transmutation, infused with the unconditional love of the Creator and magnified one thousand times by the angelic realm. Clear and dissolve all harmful energies and take them to the light. I call upon Metatron to act as my witness. Thank you, it is done."

See and feel your energy merging with the collective energy on the grid and being projected towards the Earth. See or feel the Violet Flame rising up from the Earth and merging with the light from the grid and watch as it swirls into the atmosphere around the Earth. See sparks of golden light as chemicals, toxins and gasses are transmuted by the energy. You may see or feel masters, archangels and angels of the angelic realm assisting the healing.

Hold the energy until you see, feel or know it is done. Bring your energy back into the Seventh Plane, washing yourself off in the unconditional love of the Creator. Then bring your awareness back to your body, ground back into the Earth and break your energy from the meditation and the grid.

I AM Archangel Metatron

Chapter 13
Trees: Earth's Natural Protectors

Trees are the centurions of our world. They stand guard, sometimes for centuries, producing life-giving oxygen and absorbing toxic carbon-dioxide. They provide food, shelter and resources for animals and humans alike and are both plundered and revered by the human race.

The aura of a healthy tree emits a powerful energy that radiates out to the world. Trees do much more than just hold soil in place and oxygenate the air – they emit a pure, vibrational frequency that resounds with the knowledge of the Universe. Trees are of the Second Plane of Existence, but they hold a vibrational frequency of oneness with the Creator because they just are. In the energy of the Creator everything just is and is held in the energy of unconditional love; there are no conditions or expectations of return or exchange, other than what is needed for survival. The energy emitted by the trees of the world, whether they be hundred-year old giants or one-year old saplings, is the same. They provide shelter for birds, insects and animals, oxygen and stability for the soil and take their nutrients and water from the environment that they sustain. They also provide a place of refuge for many beings, human and non-human alike. If you have ever felt the energy of a healthy tree, really felt it, the strength, power and joyful vibrations emitted would have held you in awe. Trees stand as representatives of the wonder of Creation and they can teach humans much about what it is to live a peaceful existence in total harmony and acceptance of oneself and one's environment.

Trees have a long history beyond the Earth as we know it as druids in the world of Atlantis, which was a magical yet very orderly world. The people used the laws of the Universe to their advantage, but they also honoured the natural world. They lived respectfully and sustainably for many thousands of centuries until the human ego reared its ugly head and the world of Atlantis fell. Druids were of the trees, that is, their essence came from trees, yet they lived apart from them. They were not human and were of the Second Plane, so their energies were akin to fairies and elementals. They lived by the ethos of reciprocity or everything in exchange, so what they gave out they demanded back in equal measure. They were part of the system of guardianship of the natural world and they worked symbiotically with all of the elements to maintain balance in the ecosystems of Atlantis. They lived amongst and in the trees and forests, maintaining their own territories in harmony with other plants, animals and humans. When Atlantis fell, they became immobile and their essence merged with and became one with the trees. Their guardianship of the Earth continues today.

The law of cyclic return mandates that all human life returns from death to life in a physical body to continue its soul journey to mastery. While humans continue to struggle with concepts they cannot understand beyond a physical existence, nature itself has achieved what humans strive and often fail to do, which is to exist in harmony and in symbiosis with each other, creating balance and structure. The natural world is a perfect example of mastery because, without intervention from man or other intelligent beings, it has evolved and existed for millions of years. Nature has mastered what man has not: oneness with the universe. Trees are nature's masters and must be honoured for their service.

The human consumption of wood is controversial only when it is not sustainable. Even old-growth trees that have stood for centuries must one day die and be replaced. Protected species have only become endangered through lack of respect for the environment and the human need for profit and gain, no matter the cost. It is therefore understandable that those humans who connect with and wish to protect nature would be 'up in arms' about any tree, particularly an old growth one, being destroyed for human consumption. The key to maintaining balance between the human and natural worlds does not lie

Chapter 13

in complete protection however, rather in sustainable harvesting that continues the ongoing cycle of life and death.

So, place your hand on a tree and feel its life-force resonate with yours. Its simplicity of existence is a lesson for all mankind: stand your ground and draw your strength and power from the Earth, giving back to it in equal measure. Trees, dear ones, are the finest example of oneness on Earth that you can ever hope to see amongst the chaos of the human illusion of separation.

I AM Saint Germain

Meditation Thirteen
Ground to Mother Earth

Ensure that you are sitting or lying in a comfortable position with your eyes closed. Concentrate on your breath, ensuring that, when you breathe in you fill your lungs to the top expanding your abdomen as you do. When you breathe out, expel the air slowly and gently, feeling your body relax a little more each time. Breathe in, breathe out, falling into an easy and regular rhythm, not over breathing or thinking. Your mind will wish to think, so concentrate on your breath and your body, releasing stress and tension as you go.

Focus now on your feet and feel or see a light growing around them. It is coming from Mother Earth, anchoring you and grounding your energy into hers. The light is clear and bright, soft and safe and it is moving upwards to encase your entire body. You are now completely surrounded by this light, which is protecting you and connecting you to the light of the Creator. As I say His/Her name, you become aware of a brighter light coming into your crown. This is your connection to the Divine Source. The bright, white pearlescent light moves down through your chakras, aligning, balancing and activating them to a higher vibration. It is moving down through your third eye, now your throat, your higher heart, your heart, your diaphragm, solar plexus, sacral, base and then down to your Earth Chakra.

You are now completely relaxed, grounded and connected to Mother Earth and the Creator. Continue breathing in an out and see the light that has entered your body centering in your solar plexus. You will find that you receive deeper healing and stronger energy if you begin working from

Chapter 13

there. You are still surrounded and protected by the light and love of Mother Earth and of the Creator as you breathe in and out, watching the beautiful ball of energy growing and revolving in your solar plexus. Feel the love within this ball of light – it is your love, merged with the love of Mother Earth and of the Creator.

Now, take a deep breath and hold your energy in your lungs. Feel it warm and full of life, then exhale. Breathe out all of the day's woes and negativity. When you next inhale, breathe in from your solar plexus, or your belly button. The colour is yellow. This breath will take the negative energy from that chakra and fill your lungs with it. Exhale it slowly, willingly releasing all of the tension and stress that may have built up there. Repeat twice more. Take your energy lower and breathe in from the sacral chakra, which is just below your solar plexus and is orange. Again, breathe out slowly, willingly releasing any negativity. Repeat twice more. Move further down to the red energy of your base chakra. In the next inhalation, breathe in from your base chakra, seeing the red colour and releasing the stress of the day in the outward breath. Repeat three more times.

Now, picture your feet firmly grounded into Mother Earth and breathe in her love and light, up through your feet and legs and bring it through your lungs right up to your crown. Picture Mother Earth's light joining with the light and love of the Creator and bring it back down as you breathe out again. The light and love of God and the Earth are now merging and filling your body with peace, contentment and a feeling of wellbeing. Repeat the breath from your feet to your crown and out through your lungs twice more, breathing slowly on a count of eight. You will find yourself soon fully relaxed and, if practiced daily, your chakras will remain much clearer.

I AM Saint Germain

Chapter 14
Water: The Flow of Life

The seas of the world are vast and plentiful. The life they sustain is varied and often mysterious or still unknown to humans. The separation of life between land and water means that the forms of life have different appearances, different attributes and different purposes. While all animals on Earth, whether they live on land or in the sea, feed on or are food for other animals, there seems to be no reason for their existence other than to eat, breed, sustain other life forms and to maintain the overall balance of the natural world. However, the main purpose for any life form to exist is to bring the love of the Creator to the world through its very core, which is connected to Source and is therefore created from the Adamantine Particles of Creation.

Land animals are nurtured by the sun and rain, while animals in the depths of the ocean survive with very little light and on the tiniest particles for food. Their survival is based on instinct, self-sufficiency and sustainability. If there were a lesson for humans to be learnt from sea life, from the largest whale down to the single-celled amoeba, it would be that life is not about doing. To live life on Earth, all one need do is to exist in the integrity in which it was created and to be true to itself in every second of its existence. Life in the natural world just is, and humans could do well to consider this fact.

Oceans separate landforms around the world, as do rivers and lakes and, while there is much more water than land in area across the globe, the balance between elements in different areas of the world creates different kinds of ecosystems, climates and terrains. Without the great oceans of the world, very little water would exist on the planet, as the water cycle relies on the evaporation from the seas. The importance of the tidal system around the world can also not be overlooked, as tides bring in food for the shallow dwellers and crustaceans. Without the tidal movement there would be such an imbalance in the shoreline eco-systems that many beaches would be uninhabitable. No other planet in the Universe contains oceans as vast in area or containing the diversity of life as Earth does. The oceans of the Earth are therefore extremely unique and must be protected from pollution and over-fishing. When respect is shown it will be returned; it is up to all humans on Earth to stand up for the natural world and to keep it as balanced as possible, because nature and humans are one; when one is out of balance, so will the other be.

The ebb and flow of the tides can be equated to the ebb and flow of life. What washes into the shore in one tide can be very different the next time and it cannot be controlled or planned upon. The same can be said for life. While humans can plan and save money for the future, events and circumstances can change in an instant, altering the course of one's life. These kinds of changes can either be for the better and fortuitous, or they can be devastating and heart-breaking. Whatever life brings in for you, just like the tides, has the opportunity to either stay or alter your course and the consequences of either direction may remain with you forever. The way you cope with the changes that the tide of life brings you says a lot about the experiences you have had before, what they have taught you and what you have learnt. If you see life as an endless struggle, to be survived rather than lived, then your thoughts and actions will bring more of the same. If, however, you have learnt to 'go with the flow' and to accept change as a positive force for good in your life, abundance and good fortune are likely to abound. Unlike the tides, which can be unpredictable, the Law of Attraction will always give you exactly what you project out to the Universe in your thoughts; change your thoughts, change your reality, it's really that simple.

Rivers and streams often begin in the mountains and always lead to the ocean. They bring life to the country around them as they provide food and water for animals, plants and humans alike; they are literally 'rivers of life' working in symbiosis with the environment. Similarly, the human cardiovascular system pumping blood by the heart through the veins and arteries is the human life force, or River of Life and represents the vitality and strength of each person's life-force. Any irregularity in the blood or heart, therefore, can be equated to the will and intent to live. In children with heart or blood disorders this may seem unthinkable, but the soul carries the spirit along with any trauma or karma still unresolved from past lifetimes. It is recommended, therefore, that healing be sought for the spiritual, emotional and mental bodies, not just the physical body, of the affected person if this is the case.

Lakes, unlike rivers and oceans, are still bodies of water that can go to great depths. As water represents human emotions, to dream of or be drawn to a lake can mean that your emotions run very deep. However, stillness also relates to calmness, so sitting by a lake can help to still the mind and calm any anxiety one may have. To dream of calm waters means that the worst is over, but make sure you have dealt with the emotions that could still be lying below the surface.

Water gives life and it can also take it away. To fear water is to fear tapping into your deepest emotions, because the element of water symbolises emotional balance and harmony. To dream of water in different states signifies various emotional states ranging from inner peace and calmness to raging turmoil and unrest.

Dehydration in a human will bring depression, lethargy, disconnectedness, a loss of the will to live and then death. No life form can last longer than three days without water in its system and the damage that dehydration does to the physical body is catastrophic. Considering that humans all have four bodies, only one of which is physical, one must consider how water affects the mental, emotional and spiritual bodies as well. As the human body and all other life forms are comprised of up to 80% water, the connection to creation, to nature, to the Earth and to each other is dependent on connectedness to the four sacred elements: air for the breath, earth for grounding and connectedness, fire for passion and purpose and water for emotional stability. The four sacred elements represent facets of the consciousness of the Creator which, when combined, form the essence of oneness. Bodies of water connect all elements, for fire is below the earth and air is above the water. Connection of the human spirit to the all relies on connection to all four elements most of the time in order for one to feel grounded and balanced and there is no better place than beside the ocean or a river to feel this.

The symbolism of water and reflection of the path of one's existence in bodies of water is extremely powerful and can be very useful for people who take notice of the signs presented to them in dreams and in their day to day reality. Ask me for assistance to bring the knowledge you need to the fore to bring healing and peace into past trauma and to move forward into the future.

I AM Saint Germain

Chapter 14

Meditation Fourteen
Connect to the River of Life

Breathe deeply and relax your body as you connect to Mother Earth and the light of the Creator. Feel, see or imagine a beautiful light entering your crown and connecting to your heartspace. Now, focus your energy on your physical heart, feeling the rhythmic beating of it in your chest. As you continue to focus on the weight of it in your chest, become aware of your arteries. Feel the life force pumping out into your body and merge your energy with it. How does it feel as the blood surges through: clear, fast and vital or slow and a bit sluggish? Does it match with how you are feeling energetically? Do not think it, just allow the feeling to come.

As you breathe in now, collect the beautiful light and love of the Creator through your crown and breathe it out into your heart and arteries, intending that the light clear any blockages in first your physical body, then the emotional body, which is yellow, mental body, which is blue and the spiritual body, which is violet, healing and repairing as it does so. Continue breathing slowly and regularly as you see, feel or imagine the healing occurring. Then, focus on your veins and the capillaries, breathing light and love into them, clearing, healing and repairing.

Now sit in your heart space and check in with yourself. Do you have any heavy feelings, any sadness or lingering grief that needs clearing? Are you able to say, "I love and embrace my life" without heaviness or doubt? Do you feel the love of life surging through your body, or do you feel disconnected and lost? Concentrate on your heart and the emotions it is holding, asking Creator to help you to resolve any negative beliefs and feelings about yourself and to lift past hurts and emotional trauma. As you do so, consciously breathe light and love into all of the bodies of your heart - physical, mental, emotional and spiritual, releasing negativity as you go. Feel it wash everything that no longer serves you; away with the light out through your feet. Keep doing this until you feel a change.

Now say, "I love and accept myself. I embrace my life. I am grateful for my gifts and for the abundance I have." Repeat this as often as is necessary until your sub-conscious accepts and believes it. Remember, what you project out to the Universe will come back to you in equal measure.

You are very loved.

I AM Saint Germain

Chapter 15
Mountains: The Stillpoint of Creation

Mountains are constant – they are ever unchanging in appearance. The mountains of the world are geological constructs that have formed over millions and/or billions of years. Their presence on Earth is no accident, as they are monoliths that hold vortexes of energy that penetrate deep underground linking to the energetic grid around the Earth. The top of a mountain, the apex or peak, is the smallest yet most powerful part of the mountain itself, as the energy is the strongest at the top, hence people call them 'mountain peaks'. Mountains are the epitome of the saying, "Earth meets sky," as the peak of every mountain draws the energy of Creation down into the depths of the Earth, creating vortexes and structures all the while holding the energy of the Earth in powerful stillness.

Mountains hold energy that is both ancient and new; much of it is sacred and quite a bit of it is negative. It would be better for the world if all of the negative and darker energy were released into the light due to its sinister nature. Because mountains are so solid, they hold energy in like a cave, but every rock and piece of dirt contains the energy held within. That is why it is best if humans never remove any part of a mountain – not one rock or crystal, no sand and no soil, because the energy it contains could transfer into their energy fields creating negative or even detrimental effects.

There are many crystals under the Earth that are enormous in size and which generate vibrational energy out into the world. Crystals hold and magnify energy in a way that rocks cannot and their presence around the globe is stabilizing and important to the balance of nature. Although many of them are not in the vicinity of mountains, their energy travels into vortex points, some of which is harnessed by mountainous ranges.

The awe that one feels when in a mountain's presence is not just due to its size; the power comes as much from within the mountain as it does from its exterior. The history of the world goes beyond human residence, with much of the energy still held within the depths of the Earth and inside mountains. The stillness of the mountain is its greatest strength, because the energy drawn or harnessed through stillness is powerful in nature. In fact, mountains are the epitome of the 'still-point of creation', and the magnification of energy created by this is awe-inspiring.

The Universe is vast and expansive. Between each star, planet, rock and piece of debris there is....space. Within each space there is potential for creation to occur. Mountains are stillpoints, but humans can create a stillpoint using the breath.

As each person takes a breath there is a moment in time where all is still. If you hold that breath you extend that stillpoint moment where everything just is. While it is impossible to continue holding your breath without dire consequences, it is possible to learn to be still in body and mind to create that stillpoint; that moment in time where the possibilities are endless and your connection to the all is the strongest. When the mind and body are still there is optimum opportunity for creation and manifestation because the causal body, the higher self and the sacred mind are all in sync with each other. In this moment, the sacred mind can connect with the Universal Mind through every cell in the body. Every cell contains adamantine particles which are the essence of Creation and every particle contains the Universal Mind. This mind contains universal knowledge and wisdom that every soul on Earth knows but which many have forgotten whilst in human form. To access the Universal Mind, or everyone's higher self, one must learn to just be.

The advantages of being still in mind and body however, go way beyond accessing universal information. The benefits to one's health and wellbeing when one takes the time to centre, breathe and clear one's mind cannot be underestimated, because a racing mind can cause everything to speed up and become a blur. In this state one can miss important moments in time that could potentially be much bigger, manifesting wonderful situations and opportunities, had one taken the time to notice. Also, stilling the mind and slowing one's breath immediately brings one into an alpha state, which is a slower brain wave. There is much less chance of one making rash decisions, saying harsh words or burning proverbial bridges when one slows the mind down and considers all possibilities. In the alpha state all becomes clear, rational and unmuddied. If everyone on Earth operated from the alpha state as a matter of course the world would be in an ascended state already!

So, be like a mountain and harness your spiritual power through moments of stillness that connect you more deeply to your guides and the Source of Creation. Stand in the magnificence of you and show the world who you truly are.

I AM Lord Melchizedek

Meditation Fifteen
Stillpoint Meditation

(Please Note: If creating a stillpoint is difficult for you, channel the energy of the mountains by focusing on a picture or mental image of one. Creation of any kind in a stillpoint will only happen with intention and very clear focus. Before you begin the meditation, hold the intention of what it is you wish to create in your mind's eye, asking that it be done for your highest and best and in the highest and best way. At the end of your meditation, sit for a few minutes in the stillness, give thanks for your abundance and blessings, then let go of any expectation of outcome. The Universe will answer most swiftly to those who allow themselves to be in Divine Flow.)

Focus your energy on the majesty of a mountain's energy and close your eyes. Picture a pattern that resembles a figure 8, or infinity sign, and match your breath to it on a count of 8 – breathe in two, three four and out two, three, four. Imagine the top part of the figure 8 looping up as you breathe in and the bottom part looping down as you breathe out. If you find that difficult, simply make the pattern with your hand, breathing in on the upward loop and out on the downward loop. Breathe in, 2, 3, 4 and breathe out 2, 3, 4.

Once you get the rhythm, hold your breath at the first count as you breathe in, just for a second, thus creating a stillpoint after every count of 8. Breathe in and hold, 3, 4 and breathe out 2, 3, 4. With each stillpoint that you create, send light and love into that which you wish to create and feel the love grow inside of you, filling the stillpoint and your intention with light. Breathe in and hold, 3, 4 and breathe out 2, 3, 4.

Chapter 15

Breathe in and hold, 3, 4 and breathe out 2, 3, 4. Breathe in and hold, 3, 4 and breathe out 2, 3, 4. Feel the energy of love building with each complete breath.

When your still point is filled to the brim with the bright light of Creation, focus your energy on it and hold it within your being, all the while maintaining your breath at a slow count in and out. Clear your mind and allow the stillness to fill you. You will find your breath will slow even more, your mind will clear of thoughts and your body will be relaxed and calm. You may wish to stop this recording for a time as you absorb the stillness and peace.

When you are ready, let go of that you have created in the stillpoint energy and watch it merge into the light of Creation. Bring your attention back to the room and take a moment to ground and centre your energy.

I AM Archangel Michael

Chapter 16
Crystals: Energy Healers

In the depths of Mother Earth, scattered across the globe, lie huge crystal formations which act as energy stabilizers for the natural world. Crystals are of the first dimension along with the four sacred elements of air, water, earth and fire. Their closest elemental relative is water, for without water and minerals they would not form.

Crystals can be sourced from all over the planet, but the vast formations far beneath the surface are the focus for this chapter. These crystals have been instrumental, since time began, in holding the energy of the planet stable through vibrational frequencies unique to their structures. These frequencies connect symbiotically to nature in its different forms and they can even influence the seas and the weather.

Crystals are elements of the Earth. They hold memory, often as physical form. They can trap energy and they can also transmute it. Crystals are highly powerful objects which, in the wrong hands, can become powerful weapons. They magnify energy to such a degree that they can burn and wither matter. They can also strengthen the intention of the mind through thought, meditation and prayer, which is why so many people use them when performing their energy work. The energy of crystals themselves is so powerful that, when combined with other elements such as water or fire the resulting energy can transmute and transform solid matter. Crystals have their own vibrational frequency which creates an energy unlike other rock or stone. They give off a light and a sound which changes the vibrations around them as well as absorbing lower energies.

As the energy is absorbed, the nature and strength can result in changes in the crystal's structure, often fracturing or breaking it in the process. If crystals are not cleansed of the energies they have absorbed, they become ineffectual in their ability to absorb and cleanse lower vibrational energies. It is therefore advisable for people using crystals in energy work to cleanse them after every use.

The giant underground crystals absorb and hold energy; when the Earth was uninhabited they maintained an equilibrium on Earth that existed until the industrial age. With the introduction of so many chemicals and industrial waste, not to mention household rubbish and fossil fuel emissions, the energy of the Earth has, over time, become more and more polluted and low-vibrational. As the assault on the Earth's resources and energies has increased over the centuries, the kind of energy that the crystals are now absorbing is vastly darker and denser than ever before. The impact on the stabilisation of the natural world has been devastating; not only has human kind caused the extinction of many animals, the desecration of forests, pollution of rivers, streams, oceans and the air they breathe, but the changes in atmosphere caused by emissions have caused a globalised warming that can never be fully reversed.

In the case of the huge crystal formations deep below the Earth's surface, the energies absorbed are, depending on their location, cleansed by the water table or seepage. In some cases, their restructuring as they break down acts as a cleansing mechanism in itself. In many other cases, however, the crystals have no way of eliminating the toxic energies they have absorbed, other than the Devas assigned to look after them, and even they are struggling.

All crystals contain their own deva who will look after them for the life of the stone, which could literally be centuries or aeons of time. The role of a Crystal Earth Deva is to use the Earth's sacred fire to cleanse and rebalance the frequency of each crystal within the Earth. For elementals to maintain the balance in the natural world, the symbiosis between living and non-living things must remain within a certain ratio of equanimity, purity and harmony. A slight disruption can be put to rights, but a major disruption or act of destruction causes the Devic Kingdom in that environment to become extremely distressed and angry, causing further imbalance to occur. If you can, consider the consequences that may occur, then relate them to recent natural disasters on the planet − it will then be easy to realise how important these crystals are in

Chapter 16

maintaining the equilibrium and order in the non-living and living world alike.

The giant crystals deep below the Earth's surface have been absorbing energy for eons, both positive and negative, but they have also been healed to a certain degree by the Lightworkers around the world who have thought to send toning energy to them. The Fifth Dimensional energy now being emitted from Mother Earth has had a profound effect on the vibrational pull that they are having on those who are not yet attuned with the frequencies of Ascension. Many people are feeling distinctly out of sorts and completely unbalanced due to the higher vibrations coming up from Mother Earth's centre. Because these energies are being magnified and accentuated by the crystal layers, they are discordant with the lower vibrations of the third dimension and will therefore affect anyone who has not yet begun to shed their old thought patterns, negative behaviours and past emotional trauma. If you have done some work and feel connected to Spirit but suddenly feel out of balance and ungrounded, it is extremely important for you to look for ways to cleanse, balance and ground your energies in order to become more in tune with the vibrations of Ascension.

The crystals that you use in meditation can assist you to rebalance and harmonise your energies. To choose the correct crystal for your current needs, all you need to do is to focus on how you are feeling whilst hovering your hand over your crystal collection. Alternatively, you could use a pendulum to help you to select the crystal that is right for you at the time. Crystals can be placed by your bed, under your pillow, under your bed or massage table, in your pocket or worn as jewellery. Be aware that they absorb energy readily and must be cleansed often. Also be aware that, as your energies become more balanced and in tune with those coming from Mother Earth, the type of crystals that you need may change, or your need for crystals may diminish altogether.

I AM Archangel Zadkiel

Meditation Sixteen
Crystal Healing Meditations

1. For Self

Sit comfortably, close your eyes and take a few breaths in and out to centre and relax. Then, hold the intention that you are connected to the unconditional love of the Creator with ease, grace and intelligence. Also call upon the masters of light who are to help you with this healing today for your highest and best. See, feel or know who is with you; if you cannot, acknowledge their presence and thank them for being with you. Know and trust they are there. Relax your body and your mind. Now hold the intention that you receive a crystal healing that is for your highest and best to restore you to optimum health and happiness.

Hold out your hands and ask to be given the crystals that are to be used for your healing. There will be up to eight. You may see, feel or know the shape, colour and types of crystals that appear energetically in your hands, or you may not. Now place them on your lap close to your base chakra and watch or sense each crystal fly to its corresponding chakra. Continue to breathe slowly and regularly as you focus on your chakra line, allowing the crystals to cleanse, align and balance all of your chakras, starting at the base. When the energy is above your crown it will descend through your aura, healing and sealing it down to the ground. You will then feel a grounding occur and the crystals will appear in your hands again.

Give thanks for your healing and to the masters for their assistance. Give gratitude for your health, abundance and happiness. The crystals will dissolve in your hands and *you will feel replenished and renewed. Take a moment to ground and centre your energy and break your energy from the crystals before opening your eyes.*

I AM Holy Amethyst

2. For the Earth

Holding an amethyst crystal, sit comfortably, close your eyes and take a few breaths in and out to centre and relax. When you are ready, hold the intention that you are connected to the unconditional love of the Creator with ease, grace and intelligence. Call on me, Holy Amethyst, to now assist you to send healing vibrations to the crystal formations deep within Mother Earth to bring them and all of nature back into balance.

Work to slow your breathing and relax your body as you focus on the energy of the amethyst crystal as a proxy for the crystals within the Earth. See, feel or imagine the crystals being cleansed of all negative energy through vibrational frequency, toning, heat and light. Then, see, feel or imagine the violet flame transmuting any lingering heavy or dark energy; golden sparks of light will indicate their cleansing and healing. Finally, a bright, pearlescent light fills the crystals, bringing them to a higher vibration and back into balance. You may even feel the energy in the crystal you are holding.

When it is done, send your energy down into Mother Earth and give thanks for the healing. Hold the intention that your own energies be cleared and disconnected from the crystals, then open your eyes when you are ready. Cleanse your crystal accordingly when you are finished.

I AM Holy Amethyst.

Chapter 17
The Insect Kingdom: Bees – Working Together for the Greater Good of All

Bees are the epitome of oneness as they live in colonies and all work for the greater good of the hive. The life of a bee is short but productive, with not one individual out of thousands ever claiming mastery over another. Each type of bee has its place and its job and all members of the hive work in synchronicity together.

All species of bees use the nectar of flowers to produce food for the hive. Different species of flowers have adapted over time to ensure they receive the optimum benefit from the bees' service; cross pollination and the ongoing survival of many species of plants are dependent on bees and their visitations. The symbiosis of life is never more evident than in the world of bees.

Bees are not the only insects to live in colonies, but their existence is crucial to the ongoing balance of nature on Earth. This fact is well known by scientists and environmentalists around the globe, while the habitats of many native species of bees continue to be destroyed by pollution, the devastation of natural forests, man-made chemicals and pesticides. As man continues to develop more techniques for manipulating the environment using technology, chemicals and fossil-fuelled machines, the very existence of environmentally sensitive animals such as bees and frogs are threatened. These two animals alone are man's warning signs that the habitat in which they live is clean or toxic, as neither can survive in even mildly polluted conditions.

What can bees teach humans? The hierarchical structure of a beehive is not dependent on status or degrees of social importance. The Queen Bee, for instance, does not live a life of luxury in a castle as some humans do, nor is there any less work for her to do. In fact, a Queen's job is to lay eggs with no respite, with the life of the hive completely dependent upon her; if she dies or leaves, the hive is disbanded. Although her health and wellbeing is critical for the survival of the hive, her role is one of unity, not separation, as on Earth; her presence is critical to the continuation of life and to unity in her hive, a state which is not replicated in the human world.

Status, power and privilege do nothing more than create the illusion of separation, which in turn immediately causes people of lesser rank to feel inadequate and inconsequential. These states can also serve to inflate the ego of the people born or married into royalty, which has been evident in history, but which is less evident in the service that modern royals do for charities in more recent times. In fact, many privileged people are quite ascended in their consciousness and spend their lives atoning for their status by serving the community at large. This is because all humans come from the Source of Creation, the Creator of All that Is and know only unconditional love and oneness in their ethereal state. Therefore, all people who have awakened and connected to their Christ Consciousness, no matter their status in society, will work to bridge the divide between their position and the masses. In historical times, however, many injustices were carried out by people of royal or noble status to the poor, the trauma of which many people continue to carry around in their soul memories today.

Everyone on Earth has their place, just as in a beehive, yet most people are working for their own benefit, often at the expense of other's health, wellbeing and happiness. If people were to overcome their ego to accept each other and work together no matter where they live, their status, colour, race or religion, the future of Ascension on Earth would be assured.

Sacred geometry in the human world is only a representation of the perfect DNA structure of all living species on Earth and non-living matter in the Universe. Every shape, number, letter and figure used by man can be found

Chapter 17

in the natural world. The magic of nature and the miracle of creation can be found in every flower blooming around the world. Flowers, the source of all bees' nutrition, represent sacred geometry in its most natural and perfect form. All flowers, no matter the species, are symmetrical in nature and stem from a tiny seed, a bulb or a rhizome, blooming spectacularly and perfectly according to their genetic structure. In perfect union, bees use symmetrical dances to communicate distance and direction to their fellow workers, which is another example of the wonder of nature and the miracle of life.

Geometry, then, is sacred because it stems from Creation and can be used to create either health and wellbeing or harm and destruction, depending on the intention of the user. All geometry contains light codes that can be used to raise or lower the consciousness of man. When used for healing, sacred geometry can balance, align and activate human energy to a higher frequency, allowing the person to evolve spiritually and to rise above the lower vibrations of ego and self-service. Please try the following lotus flower meditation, that uses sacred geometry to assist you to activate the light codes within your DNA structure towards a higher level of consciousness and spiritual evolvement.

I AM Yeshua ben Yoseph (Jesus).

Meditation Seventeen
Reharmonize the Body Using a Pendulum

(Sit with your feet firmly grounded and a table or flat surface in front of you. You will also need some paper, a pen or pencil and a pendulum. If you don't have one, use a necklace or anything long and weighted that has your energy in it. If you wish, you may record the direction of the pendulum after each section as this will document how much light is entering your system. We recommend a sacred geometry meditation such as this every two to three months, depending on the rate of your spiritual evolution.)

Close your eyes and take a few deep breaths, relaxing your shoulders and slowing your breaths down each time. Then, call me in, Lord Melchizedek, in the energy of the unconditional love of the Creator, to balance and reharmonize your bodies and energy fields in the highest and best way. See, feel or know my presence then focus your attention on the area of your Crown chakra.

Open your eyes now and take up your pendulum, all the while focusing on your crown with your mind. Hold the intention that all of your chakras be balanced and aligned with the symbol or symbols that are appropriate to you and hold your pendulum in front of you, keeping the hand that is holding it still. I will move the pendulum according to the clearing, aligning and balancing that is needed. There will be up to three symbols used. If the symbols become more complicated, I am activating your chakra system to a higher dimension of consciousness. This will happen the more you practice this meditation. Pause this recording until it is done.

Chapter 17

Now we will clear and align your four bodies. The first is the physical body. Hold the pendulum closely over your free hand as a proxy and watch as the pendulum works to sweep the chakra healing into your aura. Then watch as I create sacred geometrical symbols through the pendulum to balance, clear and align your body. Although it is being held over your hand, trust that the healing is happening. Wait until the pendulum stops moving.

Now focus on your emotional body. Move the pendulum up away from your hand slightly and keep it still as the pendulum clears, balances and aligns your emotional body. When the pendulum stops, bring the pendulum up further and focus on your blue mental body. When it stops, pull it up further and focus on your spiritual body, which is violet. Pause this recording until it is finished.

When all of your bodies have been healed, move your hand to spiral the pendulum in a clockwise motion above your hand, which will integrate the energy and finish the healing.

Put the pendulum down and thank me for the healing. Then hold the energy for a few moments before grounding and centering your energy.

I AM Lord Melchizedek.

Chapter 18
The Animal Kingdom: Mammals – Unconditional Love

The animal world is vast and diverse, made up of many species, both on land and in water, and it has inhabited Earth for many millions of years before man. The animal kingdom survives on instinct and the ability to adapt to its surrounding conditions. Living and non-living exist in symbiosis, natural order reigning, with the natural hierarchy of predator and prey allowing for sustainability and regeneration of food sources. At the top of the order are mammals, whose ability to think and reason allow their dominance over lesser-evolved species.

Humans are mammals and, as such, belong to the animal kingdom. Their existence has theoretically evolved from apes, as the ability to evolve and adapt to the environment applies to all species, and their journey from ape to human has been scientifically proven. On Earth, humans are considered to be more highly evolved than any other animal due to their intellectual and communicative abilities but, spiritually, nothing could be further from the truth. Generally speaking, the human race has cut itself off from its spiritual connection to Source through religious and doctrinal beliefs that have led to separation of the spiritual body from the physical form and, over the centuries the illusion of separation has literally brought the Earth to its knees.

The human spirit is evolved from Source and, as such, is only attached to the physical form through incarnation and karmic contracts. The Christ Consciousness, or the knowledge that all in the Universe is connected through unconditional love, has been reduced over the centuries to religious tokenism and the elitist view that Heaven is available to a chosen few. Since the Earth ascended in 2012, the veil of illusion continues to lift on the awakening consciousness of the masses and a spiritual evolution is taking place on a grand scale. Just as all living species upon Earth continue to evolve to adapt to changing conditions in their environment, the human body struggles to catch up to the rapid evolution of the spiritual body in response to its reconnection to its Divine Blueprint. As a result, many people who have reconnected to their own spirituality are finding themselves with physical symptoms that have no plausible cause. They may also find themselves awakening psychically and becoming more attuned to the gifts of the Universe in all their many forms. This has to happen, if the future of the Earth and human inhabitation upon it is to be secured.

All mammals have a soul which carries their spirit. This fact becomes instantly apparent, should you gaze into the eyes of a dog, a bear or an elephant, particularly when they are in distress. Any animal with a soul is on a journey of self-discovery across lifetimes and can live thousands of lifetimes across dimensions, worlds and galaxies. No soul is bound to one particular physical form or planet to learn their lessons or to carry out their service, hence it is possible, although not common, for a human soul to reincarnate as a dog or any other mammal. It is uncommon because all other mammals are ascended masters living in animal bodies to bring the unconditional love of the Creator to the world. Unless a soul has achieved mastery, it is not possible for them to take on animal form.

How then, you may ask, can a master live in animal form when animals hunt and kill for food, particularly mammals which are at the top of the food chain? Is not the body sacred? Is killing not a travesty and a sin? The answer lies in Universal Law, which states that all matter, both living and non-living, is energy which is ever exchanging and interchanging, being consumed and replaced in equal measure. The exchange of life for food gives life to the taker, which will eventually be given or taken for an exchange of food for life. The flow of energy is only interrupted when the killing is outside of these laws of exchange and the karmic cycle is immediately initiated.

Chapter 18

It is true that all life is sacred. In the eyes of spiritual law, taking a life unnecessarily is the ultimate travesty, because every living thing is loved unconditionally by the Creator and no-one individual is more important than another, whether it be an insect, a lion, a tree or a human. Furthermore, all life exists in the cycle of return and abides by the law of evolutionary expansion, which requires the application of sustainability. This means that whatever is taken for food, shelter or profit and gain must be replaced in equal measure. In the natural world animals kill other animals for food and survival. Man is, after all, an animal is he not? It is within man's rights, therefore, to kill for food to receive the balance of nourishment his body needs. However, when more is taken than is necessary, or plundered without replacing what is taken, an imbalance occurs, causing some animals to become depleted in number and in vibration. Many animals have died out altogether due to over-fishing and unsustainable hunting.

As most animal protein consumed by humans is farmed, the law of sustainability is being abided by; however, not all animals are killed for food and this is where the biggest imbalance has been created. In many countries, animals are killed for skins, tusks and organs, or kept in inhumane conditions for human benefit. There must be sustainability, but there also must be grace and respect for the life taken, in order for the vibration of the gift of life to be at its highest and nutritional best.

The vibrational nature of food is very much dependent on the nature of its breeding, its growth, its nurturing and harvesting. When blessings are not given, or the life is taken without request or respect, the vibration of the nourishment received will be of a much lower order than if the animal had been killed with love, thanks and blessings. If an animal has been bred with love and care, with all its needs being respected and its very presence honoured, the nature of its nutrition after death will be much higher than the products that come from animals raised in low-vibrational conditions. When animals are bred from a vibration of income, greed and ego, the vibration of the food will be of a much lower order, particularly if the animal suffered in any way, including animal products such as eggs.

All life is sacred and equal. As already mentioned, spiritual law allows animals to kill other animals for food, as long as they kill for need, not for the sake of killing. Do not fear the act of killing for food if that is what is required to maintain your health. Be conscious, however, of the consequences of taking life and consuming or using it without gratitude or its permission. By giving thanks and love to the animal who has given its life to sustain yours, you are balancing the exchange of energy, both for you and for the species of animal from which you take. It is entirely possible to do this in retrospect if you have no control over how the animal's life was taken, such as when you buy meat or animal products from the supermarket. All you need to do is to visualise light going into the food and consciously give thanks and blessings for the gift of nutrition that it is giving to you. If you are doubtful of the origin of the product you can also intend that the energy of the food be raised to its highest and best, so it is of the most benefit to your health and well-being.

Survival on Earth in the physical form is dependent on food, water, warmth, light and love; no human on Earth should be without those requirements. However, sustainability and balance are vital in keeping the Earth's natural world working symbiotically and in harmony. The vibration in which you live is the vibration you attract. Take only what you need and always be grateful to the animal that was sacrificed so you can live.

Blessing

The Christian practice of saying Grace before a meal serves as a blessing for the food and an expression of gratitude for the gift of life for one's health and wellbeing. Here is a simple blessing for you to use before eating any food that has come from animals.

"Mother, Father God, Creator of All That Is, I give thanks and gratitude to the animals who have given their life for my nutrition. I hold the intention that this food be filled with your light and unconditional love and that its vibration be raised until it is of optimum benefit to my ongoing health and wellbeing. Thank you, it is done, it is done, it is done."

I AM Lord Melchizedek

Chapter 18

Meditation Eighteen
The Sacred Breath

To breathe is to live. The breath is sacred because every breath connects you to the sacred element of air and grounded to the sacred element of earth. All life is sacred because every living thing has been created in the energy of unconditional love which is the energy of Source and creation itself. Your body, therefore, is also sacred and should be viewed as the ultimate temple to be nurtured and revered. Every breath you take is nurturing your body and, with intention, will keep you connected to the Source of life and creation. Today we will use the breath to restore balance in our bodies and to reconnect our consciousness to the beauty we hold within.

Find a quiet and comfortable place to sit or lie down. Take some steady breaths until you feel yourself relaxing. Slow your breath to a count of four breaths in and four breaths out, ensuring that you fill your lungs completely and exhale completely, extending your abdomen as you do so.

Become aware of your heart space in the middle of your chest area and focus your attention on it. Feel your energy building there as a beautiful ball of pearlescent, white light, all the while keeping your breathing slow and steady. Now, on an outbreath, send your ball of light down through your chakras, down through your legs and deep down into Mother Earth, sending light-roots into the earth and grounding yourself there. Then, breathe in and bring your energy back up, through your feet, through your legs and up through all your chakras until it is in your crown at the top of your head. Hold it there while breathing in and out on a count of four and imagine a light coming into your crown and connecting to your light. This is the light of Creation. Bring this energy back down into your heart space and feel the light spreading around you until you are totally immersed in it.

Become aware of your lungs and focus all of your attention on them as you begin to regulate your breathing. Breathe in counting slowly to six and out on a count of six. Breathe in two, three, four, five, six and out two, three, four, five, six. Feel the air fill your lungs as you expand your abdomen, giving life to your body; breathe out slowly, expelling the air completely.

On the next breath, breathe in the air as the light of Creation, filling your lungs with unconditional love. Each time you breathe in feel the light expand from your lungs out into every part of your body until your body is ablaze with the Light of Creation. When you breathe out, intentionally expel any physical illness or ailment you may have in your body. Breathe in the unconditional love of Creation and breathe out illness, sickness and pain. Every time you breathe, focus the inbreath on the area of pain, illness or discomfort, filling it with the healing light of unconditional love, then consciously breathe out all that does not serve you. Breathe in, breathe out. Breathe in, breathe out. If you need more time, stop this recording until all is released.

Now we will focus on the emotional trauma that has accumulated over time. Still focusing on the illness or pain in the body, feel the emotions and trauma behind them and fill them with the unconditional Light of Creation. Breathe out and send the emotions out to the light to be gone forever. Continue to do this until you feel a release. Again, you may wish to stop this recording until it is done.

Now focus on your mind, breathing in the unconditional love of the Creator to clear your mind of negative thoughts,

Chapter 18

beliefs and mindsets. Bring up old thought patterns, fill them with light then breathe them out of your mind and send them to the light of Source, gone forever. Keep going until all the old thoughts are gone.

Now bring in new thoughts, ones that you have had trouble believing. With each thought, fill it with the light of Creation, but when you breathe out, send it through your body and into every cell. Think it, breathe it, believe it. I am beautiful, I love myself, I am worthy, I am important, I accept myself, I am loved, I am loveable. I AM who I AM. Whichever thought or belief is applicable to you, say it, breathe light into it, then breathe it out into your being until it becomes more believable. Stop this recording until it is done.

Finally, breathe life and love into your heart, fill it with the unconditional love of Creation to heal old wounds and hurts. Breathe in love and breathe out the darkness until it is all gone. Say, "I love, I am loved, I AM."

Use your breath now to ground back into Mother Earth and to centre yourself in your heart space. Continue to say, "I love, I am loved, I AM." When you are ready, open your eyes.

What affirmation will you make to retrain your subconscious mind? Write it and put it somewhere so you can retrain your thinking. Say it often until you believe it. Be in the light, be the light for others and show the world that anything is possible, if you believe it to be so.

I AM yours in love, light and oneness, Mother Mary.

Chapter 19
As Free as a Bird

Birds of flight are known to have a freedom that many humans envy. To soar above the heavens and to go wherever one wishes is a gift that no human can execute unaided. While many bird species live in flocks and congregate together, some are loners and navigate their lives on their own. Birds of prey, such as the eagle, are examples of this, although some species mate for life and return to the same nest each year. Birds are generally territorial and live within a limited range of their designated territory. While some live in the same habitat all year around, many migrate to breed each year. While there are many similarities between species, there are also many differences. The same can be said of humans - there are many similarities yet many differences that make each individual unique.

Birds live on instinct and in harmony with the natural world. Their habits are genetic, instinctive and regular; for instance, they rise at sunrise and go to bed when it is dark; they search for the same food and nest in the same places – they are true creatures of habit. Unlike mammals, birds do not contain a soul, but they do have a spirit which can give them certain personal characteristics within their own species. Domesticated birds, such as parrots, cockatoos and budgies are well known for developing personalities of their own through interactions with their owners, but even wild birds, such as magpies, have been recorded as developing relationships with people who feed and interact with them.

The question to be asked here is if it is within spiritual law to keep birds captive in a cage as a pet? The quick answer would be no, because the law of freewill would decree that no-one can intervene on the freedom of another, even insects and birds. However, the fact that many birds are social by nature and thrive on social and personal interaction makes it understandable that many humans keep birds as pets and enjoy their company. It is also a fair statement that many domestic birds are well loved and cared for, living comfortable and happy lives, particularly if they know no other life than within a cage. However, the enjoyment of having a pet, bird or otherwise, at the expense of the freedom of those held captive is on the threshold of transgressing spiritual law, if the conditions of captivity are inhumane or deprive the animal of their basic needs.

There is no doubt that the study of the natural world in all its forms has assisted humans to come to many wonderful scientific and medical discoveries that have benefitted all species living upon the Earth. The captivity of animals for human enjoyment, such as in zoos and circuses, is widely accepted on Earth, but also widely condemned. While the educational aspect of animal study through captivity can be justified, if any animal, including humans, are kept captive or experimented on in a way that is cruel, distressing or harmful, this transgression can only create karmic consequences. If animals and birds must be kept captive, the conditions and intentions behind their captivity will create the reality for all involved. We urge that all life be held in the utmost regard of kindness and compassion at all times.

If birds in flight are seen to be free and their ability to fly anywhere is envied by humans, why is this so? Freedom in the human world is conditional on many things, including age barriers, financial capacity, work commitments, location, and government regulations. While people in the western world may generally have more services and opportunities available to them for travel, poor financial and social status can limit opportunities for many as much as for those in less developed countries. For many, social equality is a dream that can never be fulfilled and financial freedom to live or travel wherever they please is unlikely to be realised in their whole lifetime. So, while people live freely within society, freedom to travel is a luxury that many simply cannot afford.

Spiritual freedom will come to those who can see beyond the illusion of separation and that all in the Universe is connected through the energy of love. When one can truly love themselves and accept that they are one with the all and that every living thing is loved unconditionally in the energy of all-that-is, the wonders of the Universe and all that it offers will open up to them. People who are awakened to their own divinity become more able to send love to those they no longer align with, to accept people regardless of their beliefs and to allow all people to traverse their own path without judgement or condemnation. The truth of the Universe cannot be found in religious doctrine or personal belief, yet the right to believe or not should be a freedom for all on Earth without interference by those who think their beliefs are superior, as is the case for many religions and cults on Earth.

All living beings have free will, which is a gift of Creation and to be used at each person's discretion. Free will does not give humans the freedom to choose to act at the expense of other people's free will, and all living things on Earth reside within spiritual law. Freedom of action according to law and within a person's right to do so can sometimes be restricted by other factors such as being emotionally tied to another person in a relationship, not having the resources to act at that time or being told by another that it is not possible. When one makes a decision according to their free will, the positive or negative effects of that action will ripple out to those around them and can have a greater impact than they may realise. In exercising one's free will, one must examine the cause and effect impact the action or reaction will have on themselves, their loved ones and the wider community. Once it is done or said it cannot be undone or unsaid.

How free are you in your life to be the person you know you are and to do the things you want to do? Do you allow yourself to be trapped within the limitations of your human body and the physical world, denying yourself the power to manifest your dreams into reality? Are you creating a reality that is closing in on itself when all you need to do is to believe that anything is possible?

When birds fly, they never doubt that they can. They live in the moment, never worrying about the past or the future. They live in harmony with nature and follow their built-in instincts – they know what to do because it is innate. It is time for you to remember that you are an ethereal, spiritual being having a human experience. The human spirit remembers only love and the soul knows the lessons it has chosen to learn. It also knows the difference you wanted to make in service to others. Your higher, or Christed self is the bridge to the highest consciousness of the Divine – unconditional love and oneness with all. Every person on Earth is a spoke of the wheel of Creation. Do you love yourself enough to break the ties that are binding you to a life that is not worthy of you? Try the meditation that follows to learn the feeling of unconditional love and how it feels to be worthy and loved without conditions or judgement from others.

I AM Archangel Michael.

Chapter 19

Meditation Nineteen
Rebuild Self-Love and Feelings of Worthiness

Focus in on your heart space and breathe consciously on a slow count of four breaths in and out, visualising light building in your heart space until it has totally surrounded you. Breathe in, breathe out, pushing the light further out around your body each time.

Remaining aware of yourself grounded to Mother Earth and present in the chair or on the bed, watch as the light around you turns pink, enveloping you in a cloud of unconditional love. Continue to breathe in and out slowly, until you see, feel or imagine yourself sitting on a thousand-petalled white lotus flower, surrounded by the beautiful pink light of love. Slowly, the lotus flower comes up to fold around you until you are totally encased within it. At the same time, the pink light of love is absorbed into your heart space, filling your chest with the most beautiful feeling of love, of being loved, of peace, bliss and oneness.

Now bring your focus to the areas of your belief system about yourself. Can you say, "I love you," to yourself and believe it? Can you look into the mirror and not cringe? Can you accept who you are and where you are in your life? Do you feel worthy? As you breathe, choose one of the questions and focus on that.

Bring your awareness to the colour green that is surrounding you, which is my presence. I am here to help you to shed the negative feelings you have about yourself. All you need to do is to give me, Archangel Raphael, permission to help *you to learn to feel love and acceptance for yourself and what it feels like to feel worthy of being loved. Say it now, "I give you permission, Archangel Raphael, to help me to learn how to feel love and acceptance for myself and to feel worthy of being loved."*

The lotus flower now becomes angel wings, gently cradling you as your heart, mind and body are healed with my green light, which is filled with the unconditional love of the Source of Creation and underlit with the pink colour of love. Feel the energy change as you say, "I love and accept myself," over and over until it sounds and feels more believable. You may feel a release from one of your chakras, your energetic bodies or from your physical body. See or feel the beautiful light of the Creator enter your crown and flood your body with the beautiful, warm feeling of unconditional love. Stay in this space until you feel completely calm and relaxed. You may wish to stop this recording for a time.

As the angel wings unfold and the lotus flower is again underneath you, bring your awareness back to your surroundings. Give thanks for your guidance, protection and abundance and stay still for a moment in the feelings of love bliss that will remain with you for the rest of the day. Repeat this meditation as many times as you need to help to strengthen your self-love and acceptance.

I AM yours in love and light,

Archangel Raphael.

Chapter 20
A Bird's Eye View of Climate Change

The phrase 'a bird's eye view' is well known and used in many contexts by humans. If humans could look upon the world from above as birds do, how would they see it? Remembering that birds view the world objectively and through a lens of basic need, how can humans use this viewpoint to change their perspective of life on Earth? Is the Earth a place to be cherished and respected by all who live upon her, or is it a human's right to plunder the natural resources for profit at the expense of flora, fauna and natural resources? Is climate change a fallacy, as many leaders would have the world believe, or are carbon emissions and the clearing of millions of acres of forest really causing the warming of the atmosphere at an alarming rate?

If an eagle looks down to spy its prey in a forest that has just been cleared, it will solve the problem by moving further afield. However, if man continues to clear natural habitat without thought for the food chain that exists within it, the consequences will eventually not only affect the animals and ecosystems but entire biomes. This has already happened in many parts of the world, resulting in the extinction or near extinction of many animal and plant species, destruction of habitat causing devastating salination and erosion of land, and carbon emissions that have had catastrophic effects on climates around the world. How long can Mother Earth sustain such assault? The truth is, not for long enough.

So, look now at the world you live in using the bird's eye perspective and through the lens of survival. See yourself as part of the ecosystem of the environment in which you live and consider the affect you and your neighbours are having upon the Earth. Do you have everything you need to survive? Do you live sustainably? Are you helping to conserve the environment and living respectfully, or have you forgotten how precious the Earth is in your everyday interactions?

The warming of the Earth has been a gradual process, beginning when the first emissions hit the atmosphere in the late 1700s. The Earth began warming much more steadily in the 1950s and 60s, with a sharp rise in temperatures in the last two decades. The pollution of the atmosphere is nothing new, but the calibre of the chemicals, toxins and poisons within them over the decades have caused an escalation of their destructive effect on the ozone layer and on the weather cycle. The fact that no government will fully acknowledge global warming and climate change does not mean they are not a reality – heads in the sand hide nothing. It is time for action, and quickly; in some areas of the globe it is already too late.

Birds may fly south for the winter, but soon the temperature will be just as warm there as it is from whence they came. As the polar caps melt and the seas rise, the incidents of earthquakes, volcanic eruptions and extreme weather conditions increase, human and animal lives and habitats alike are seriously at risk. The ways of life of the past cannot continue if humans wish to continue existing on Earth. Whilst the balance of energy remains on the edge of chaos, only chaos will reign!

The claim that climate change is not the only cause of global warming has merit, because the law of physics dictates it. The sun itself is increasing in temperature as it continues along its path towards burning out; the population on Earth has increased dramatically over the past century; and the Earth's orbit has shifted ever so slightly, having a dramatic effect on the stability of the polar caps. In addition, the huge crystals underneath the earth have splintered and cracked, changing their frequencies and causing other large shifts deep underground. The cycles of evolution would continue with or without man, but as humanity evolves, so it is that the impact of his technological advancement increases. Overall, the sum contribution of humanity on climate change is not far below 100%. With every single percent of human impact on the Earth's climate, the ramifications inexplicably and devastatingly increase. Climate change may be a political football in many countries and across continents, however, let the debate about the cause of climate change cease! This is only wasted energy. What is urgently needed now is practical, positive action towards stopping and reversing the effects of climate change on the planet.

There is much you can do individually to help the Earth's plight. Yes, of course, reduce, reuse and recycle, reduce emissions and lobby those in power to listen, but you can assist much more powerfully through your spiritual connection to the All. Sending love and healing energy to Mother Earth herself has never been more important, as her imbalances are sending every system existing upon her into a state of chaos. Praying for rain to quench the bushfires is not enough! Mother Earth herself needs healing. The following two meditations are powerful ways to send healing to the planet with positive intention and love.

WE ARE The Masters of the Cosmic Council

Meditation Twenty
Send Healing Energy to the Planet and Humanity

Close your eyes. Take a few breaths to centre yourself and to feel yourself connected to the earth. Imagine a beautiful white light with golden flecks descending around you as you breathe, cleansing, grounding and protecting you. This is Divine energy and will protect you throughout this meditation.

Divine energy is unconditional love. To be in this energy gives a feeling of being totally loved; you feel peaceful, calm and in a state of bliss. If you need healing, hold the intention that the light heals and protects you and see, feel or imagine it happening. Stay in this energy until you are ready to share this love with the world.

In your mind, hold the intention that love and healing be sent to Mother Earth to rebalance her energies and to realign her to the natural world. Now, in your mind's eye, see the world in front of you surrounded by a ring of energy, which represents the Universal Collective Consciousness. Gathering the light and love of the Creator's energy, which is surrounding you, project it towards the Earth and watch as it fills the globe and the collective energy, all the while holding the intention that Mother Earth be rebalanced and realigned in her energies. Imagine wrapping your arms around her and giving her a warm, loving embrace. Tell her how much you love and appreciate her while still projecting Divine love to her. Feel, see or imagine as her energy becomes lighter.

Now focus on the Universal Collective Consciousness, projecting light and unconditional love into it. See, feel or imagine the light sweeping through the collective energy, healing hatred, anger and negativity and changing it to love, patience, understanding and tolerance. Hold the intention that the violet light of forgiveness permeate the darkest parts of the consciousness and hold the energy until it looks or feels lighter.

Now focus on healing areas of the world affected by natural disasters. Hold innocent people and animals in your mind as you send light and unconditional love to help them heal. You can also ask that all souls lost in the disasters in every time, place and dimension, be offered soul release and guidance as they move forward in their soul journey. Then do the same for the countries, cities, rural areas and communities that have been affected, sending healing to the trees, plants, waterways, mountains… be as global or as specific as you wish.

Now give love to yourself. Hold yourself in the warm embrace of the Divine. Say, "I am loved, I give love, I receive love, I Am love Divine." See the light as it turns deep golden and feel your heart expand.

When you are ready, bring your awareness back to the room. Allow the light to recede and feel yourself completely present in your body. Break your energy from the world by brushing your hand through your chakras and then zipping up your aura. Ground your energy down into Mother Earth.

Remember, love is the only energy that is real.

I AM Archangel Metatron

Part 3

Embodying Your Spirituality

Chapter 21
The Attack on the World

In 2020, Illness has swept the globe and many people have died. Many countries have gone quickly into financial recession, with some countries gaining power while others flounder. Will the Earth recover? Is there hope for the future?

The world is under attack, and many people are living in fear and dread. However, not all is as it seems nor is it as bad as it may feel on the surface. Whilst it may seem that the new wave of terrorism is Covid-19, the real culprit is fear itself, for people are much easier to control when they feel that their lives are at stake.

Despite doubt, this global attack did not happen by chance and equates to chemical warfare. There have been many mistruths and smoke-shields thrown out by the media and the instigators alike, but the masses are awakening and can no longer be manipulated as much as has been the case in the past.

Great change is upon the Earth and nothing will or can be as it was. This is not to be feared, for the changes will bring about many blessings, despite the losses that have been incurred, for which we send our condolences and comfort. It is time to shed the fear and any anger you may feel at the terror that has been unleashed on the world, for the only saviour of the world is love which can only be expressed when the fear is vanquished. It is time for the old ways of doing, believing and being to be released. Many people talk about the 'new normal,' but let us tell you this – if humanity were to remain on its current path it would be writing its own death warrant. Ascension has been ongoing for much longer than was projected because so many people have ignored the signs. Enough is enough. It is time for change.

Any change comes from necessity, because nothing can change unless the old patterns of behaviour are released. The intent to change must come from the heart and mind, not just one or the other. For instance, a person can know that they need to make a change yet never follow through because their heart is just not in it. On the other hand, a person can really want to make a change but their mind holds them back through fear, belief, or lack of it. Only when the heart and mind are aligned will a person be able to truly embrace change with intention, purpose and determination.

So it is with the ascension of the planet at this great time. Never before has there been such an awakening of the masses and an urgency felt by so many that change is necessary and so imminent. With lockdown still at hand in many cities around the world at the time of writing, the loss of freedom has brought about an epiphany for many that life on Earth is a gift not to be wasted. When the playground of Earth was not available for play, the reality that life as we know it must change finally made itself felt.

What has this pandemic been about you may ask? Is it retribution for human behaviour that discounts the cost of human life above ego? Or is it a slap on the wrist from Mother Earth for mistreating her so badly? Perhaps it is a warning of the possibilities of infection and how life on Earth could be decimated by disease so easily?

In the energy of duality and separation from the Source of Creation, it is all of these things. However, in the energy of Oneness and unconditional love - the highest source of energy - it is merely a consequence of the choices humans make with their free will. These choices fly against spiritual law and create karma as well as dis-harmony, dis-equilibrium, dis-connection and distance amongst souls whose spirits are all one with the light of Source. The ramifications of being disconnected from the unconditional love of Creation to a soul are many, including dis-ease, social imbalance and a world that is so far from the Christ Consciousness of love, tolerance and peace that it cannot continue to exist in the way it has been in the past. Low vibrations of ego such as self-service, hatred, fear, revenge and anger will only manifest more of the same, making the physical body much more susceptible to succumbing to disease, illness or imbalances in the many systems and functions of the body.

Any illness or pain in the physical body has emotional links and ties to past trauma. The pandemic sweeping the globe is born out of ego, hatred and spite and fed by a wave of panic akin to those in days gone past. However, the difference now is that the media and the internet carry and spread lies, fake news, falsities and fear - mongering faster than they spread information and truth. At this moment, truth and lies are mixed up in a soup that is confusing with has an energy like treacle, which will ensnare people and keep them chained to the lower vibrations, should they allow it.

Lockdown was a necessary part of the changes that are now afoot. As with any transition, there had to be an integration of the past into the present followed by a releasing of negativity, toxicity and anything else that will no longer be of use in the consciousness of mankind. This does not happen overnight, Dear Ones! The most important message in all of this is to release fear and to embrace your Divinity. Heed the call of awakening and resist no longer. The hour is at hand and the clock is ticking.

The word 'corona' means 'crown' in Spanish. Whether the virus has infected individuals or not, the resulting mass disconnection from the Creator of All That Is and His/Her unconditional love in those who have succumbed to the fear means that the virus has lived up to its name. It has attacked the Crown chakra of these people and shut down their spiritual defences. Let me explain the significance of this attack.

Connection to the Source of Creation gives humans access to their spiritual, etheric body and to the knowing that all in the world is connected by universal love. This knowing is the saviour of the human spirit, which would otherwise be grounded in physical realities and anchored to third dimensional energy without respite. When the spirit remembers its connection to the light and love of Source, it will act as a spark of hope in the consciousness of the individual, leading the person to meditate, connect to the light and to seek out higher guidance with positivity and hope. Without this connection, all hope can seem lost and the tendency for the person to sink into fear, anger and similar toxic emotions will be a far greater threat.

So, take the time to reunite yourself with your own company and reacquaint yourself with your loved ones. Meditate, pray and play! Embrace the world as your cocoon as you integrate the energies of Ascension into your heart, mind, consciousness and Being – The Emergence has already begun.

Darkness is the opposite of the light and light will always extinguish the darkness. Look no further than the light within yourself, Dear Hearts, which is love; love for yourself, the love of your family and love for life here on Earth, because therein lies the hope for the future. When you connect to the love in your heart with selfless intention, you automatically connect to the unconditional love of the Creator, Mother/Father God, whose light is always within you and whose love for you is ever eternal.

Now is the time to take notice of the loving guidance around you and to become much more diligent in your spiritual practices. Take extra care that your thoughts and words reflect positivity and love, because any lower energies around you can only take hold if your energies match theirs. Bring in as much light as you can so you can raise your energies out of the Third Dimension and become another important light for the world.

WE ARE Lord Sananda and Lady Nada

Chapter 21

Meditation Twenty One
Absolve Fear Stemming from the Third Dimension

Close your eyes and make yourself comfortable. Take a few, slow breaths in and out and become mindful of how your body is feeling. On each outbreath, feel your shoulders relaxing and your body becoming heavier in the chair. Begin to focus on your breath, counting four breaths in and four breaths out, until you have a regular rhythm. Breathe in, two, three, four and out, two, three, four. Breathe in, two, three, four and out, two, three, four. Focus entirely on your breath and on relaxing your body.

Now see, feel or imagine a beautiful white light with golden flecks descending around you as you breathe, cleansing, grounding and protecting you. This is the light of Creation and will keep you safely protected throughout this meditation.

As you continue breathing regularly in and out on a slow count of four, see, feel or imagine a light entering your crown and descending through your chakras, anchoring you into Mother Earth. As you focus on this light, see an Angel appear in front of you as a beautiful beam of golden light. As the Angel becomes more visible, you are drawn into you his/her energy, which immediately gives you the most beautiful feeling of being loved and safe.

In this energy the angel now begins to gently draw any fear, anxiety, negativity and anger that has been blocking your chakras and energy fields from healing the past from your chakras, aura and bodies. As you watch, the Violet Flame of Transmutation enters your aura and transmutes all of this energy into golden rays of light, which are absorbed by the Golden Angel. You can contribute to this healing by willingly letting go of any resentment, grudges, guilt, grief or blame for yourself and others and releasing them into the flame, which will subside when all of the discordant energy has been healed.

The Golden Angel now invites you to breathe in the sparkly white Adamantine Particles of Creation while allowing him/her to align and balance your chakras. When they have become more centred, each chakra begins to glow more brightly as the Angel aligns them to your Higher Self and to the Divine. Continue to see, feel or imagine the beautiful particles of creation filling your lungs and thus your entire Being with love and light, leaving you in a state of bliss while the healing is completed.

See now in your mind's eye a staff being placed into your hands by the Golden Angel. This gift represents strength through connection to the love and light of Source and is to remind you that only love is real. Any time you feel yourself being drawn into the lower vibrations of fear, anger and negativity, call upon the Staff of Strength to appear. It will emit the Violet Flame and absorb all of your worries, fears and anxieties, allowing you to remain calm and to keep your consciousness above the drama of the Third Dimension.

Place your staff in your heart space; it can be used any time as a way of connecting to your higher knowing and to Divine Love.

As the light of the Golden Angel recedes, thank him/her for their presence, for their healing and gift today. Write down some affirmations to help you to remain positive and make meditation with your staff a daily or weekly practice.

I AM The Creator of All That Is.

Chapter 22
Regaining Your Voice

In 2020, the world erupted in anger at the brutality and killing of black American people. This was nothing new. Protest has, in the past, caused a stir, but not a lot has changed over time in the psyche of humans who treat certain cultures, races and genders with disrespect, hatred and inequality.

While intentional brutality against any human goes against human rights and spiritual law, the aggressive and emotional reaction across the world has actually inflamed matters rather than helping. Such anger will only serve to create more hatred and to accelerate the feelings of segregation amongst different groups of people. How can this serve humanity or create positive and sustained change? What has happened over the centuries against people deemed to be different, lesser or unworthy by certain cultures and religions is not acceptable, but how people react to any situation will either create more of the same, low vibration or begin to create positive change, depending on their perspective and demeanour.

People who rule by fear look for weakness. Once they find a way to manipulate and control individual, groups, races or whole countries, the grip they have on their minds grows ever stronger causing greater disempowerment and loss of independence and sovereignty that allows for greater manipulation and control. Those who become rich and powerful at the expense of the free will of others risk not only invoking the wheel of karma but also of making their journey towards enlightenment and master many lifetimes longer and much more difficult.

The vibration of the energy that you project out to the world immediately invokes the Law of Attraction and will be delivered back to you in the same vibration. So, if you are sending out negativity, that is what you will attract back. The more negative you are, the harder it will be for you to feel any kind of love or joy, bringing about feelings of loneliness, abandonment, poverty and depression. You may be abundant, but happiness comes from within, not from how much you own. Maintaining a positive outlook and doing your best to emit love and joy, appreciation and gratitude, even in the face of adversity, will allow the Universe to deliver the same vibrations back to you in spades. It is much easier to see a way out of a harsh reality when your countenance is positive.

Those in power will always seek to oppress through violence, fear and domination, but the only way to change this behaviour is through disengagement from the energy in every way. Taking a step back means that you can allow yourself to view what is happening without feeling emotionally involved. Once the emotion is removed, any response you make will be more considered, more purposeful and much more powerful.

Disengagement does not mean you do nothing! If one of your family is murdered or you are a victim of a crime, of course you will feel angry, scared or sad and you will be justified in the desire to bring the perpetrator/s to justice. However, allowing the low vibrations to drag you down to the level of the perpetrators' is not the answer and will only fuel the fire, making the problem worse, possibly even putting your own health and wellbeing in danger.

What can you project out to the world that is pure in its essence and of the highest vibration of light? Love is the only energy that transmits a frequency high enough to transcend the weaker and denser vibrations of the Third Dimension. Love is always the answer, even if it is hard to forgive those who have done so much wrong. How can you act in the energy of love whilst holding those who have overstepped the mark to account?

Speaking your truth with love will always hold much more power than if it is fuelled by angry emotions. Holding your ground with silent determination and empowerment will be much more deafening than any violent protest. Loving yourself enough to remove yourself from the energy all together is the most powerful thing you can do, as it will give you space to consider all your options before speaking. It may be the most important thing of all, because

Chapter 22

actions on the wings of emotion will never be as effective and could just result in a larger sacrifice of energy on all counts.

Standing up in the face of oppression has caused many people their lives. It is one thing to do so in a country that permits freedom of expression, but in countries that rule as a dictatorship, as a communist rule, or in a country that is dominated by the male ego, speaking up and out is dangerous. For many under communist rule, a dictatorship, or women who are oppressed through their culture and religion, freedom is a dream that haunts them in their sleep. For people who struggle with poverty, loneliness, domestic violence or mental health issues, the darkness may seem overwhelming. It is time to for change, but the change must come within you before it can begin to change externally.

For people who are not given a voice and who seemingly have no choices available, I speak to you now. As small as you may feel, you matter. In the energy of the Universe where every single thing is united through the unconditional love of Source, you are equally as important as anyone else. You matter and your voice counts. I honour you and I encourage you to begin fighting your situation in the only way possible – through prayer, meditation, the giving of gratitude for what you have and the sending of love to your oppressors. While this advice may seem abhorrent to you, I urge you to do it for a month without judgement or hesitation and keep a journal of it. Do it every day and I guarantee it will turn your life around. There is always a choice, even when it may seem there isn't.

When you make changes to yourself, the world changes around you. When you can be more at peace with what you cannot change, you will feel less anxious, fearful and stressed and become much clearer about what is happening to you. Take time to consider all sides and take back your power. Pray, meditate and find your inner calm. Call for help and we will answer you. Feel our love and your will never feel alone again. There is a way, and it is called 'Love'.

I AM Master Afra.

Meditation Twenty Two
Meditate for Inner Peace

Sit in a quiet place and connect to the Earth through your base chakra. Send your energy as light into the Earth, grounding through light roots that anchor your energy safely. At the same time, feel your connection to the light and love of God, the Creator, through your crown. Give thanks for your life, the love in your life, for your health, your wealth and your freedom. Centring your energy in your heartspace, thank the Universe and God for helping you to change your and your family's situation as if it has always happened. Give thanks for helping your oppressors to learn their lessons and hold the intention that they learn what unconditional love feels like.

Ask now for help to be strong in the face of all your challenges and feel a swell of energy in your solar plexus. Allow all fear to be swept from your body as the Creator's light strengthens you within.

Now ask to be able to feel forgiveness, to be reconnected to universal love and empowered to find peace within. Hand all of your worries and fears for the present and future, plus all of the anger from the past, over to God and the Universe as you see, feel or imagine the Violet Flame of Transmutation enveloping you, taking all of your fears, anger and lack of forgiveness away. Then, as the Flame subsides, feel the energy of the Creator filling your Being with pure light. Your body relaxes and becomes warm, calm and you feel a complete inner peace.

When you feel calm and can feel God's love within you, begin to send it out to the world as a beautiful blanket. Call *for the masters to infuse this blanket with the Violet Flame of Transmutation and to wrap the outside world in this energy. Ask that all of the fear, anger, hatred and oppression in the Human Collective Consciousness be cleansed and transmuted to love and sent back to the Earth in the highest and best way, by the Law of Grace. There must be love in your intention and in your heart as you do this.*

When you feel it is done, let go of any attachment to the healing and bring your attention back to your body. Centre your energy once more in your heartspace and breathe slowly while you sit in the sanctity within. When you are ready, open your eyes.

You are always enough.

I AM Master Afra.

Chapter 23
The 11:11 Ascension Portal

Many people report seeing repeated numbers and taking them as meaningful signs and guidance from their guides. However, with new activations underway to push the Earth and humanity to a higher state of consciousness, the messages behind repeated numbers are important to interpret.

The Ascension Portal is open and the invitation to enter it is given as the numbers 11:11. If you are repeatedly seeing this number combination, you are ready for the next phase in your spiritual evolution. The symmetry of this master number represents the columns of ascension with the colon a symbol of polarity – as above, so below. The Ascension Portal is the new activation available to those souls who have risen sufficiently in their consciousness to stay above the lure of third dimensional energy, which is heavy in density and stifles spirituality. Now is the time to answer the call to go through the portal on your journey to becoming a wayshower and mentor for others.

If you are also seeing other numbers repeatedly, the messages behind them are as equally important to uncover, because your ability to receive this new activation depends upon clearing any blockages that have been holding you back. We, the masters of light, are ever here to assist you to achieve your dreams and to be the very best you can be. All we need is permission from you to help you in your quests.

1111 adds to the number 4 which equates to the heart chakra. The activation received when entering the new Ascension Portal is one of unconditional love and an instant healing of any lower energies that may still be present within your four bodies. If, however, you see the number 4 repeatedly in any combination, it is an indication that a blockage exists in your heart chakra that needs your awareness, recognition and attention.

All numbers up to 7 can be attributed to the main seven chakras. 11 before them means that the Ascension Portal awaits you but there is work to do to clear major emotional, mental or spiritual blockages in the chakras indicated by the numbers. So, 11:47 indicates the heart and crown chakras, 11: 56 means blockages are present in the throat and third eye. If you add 4 and 7 or 5 and 6 they make 11, so when the blockages are cleared, the 11:11 portal will be ready to receive and activate your chakras to enter the galactic gateway, represented by the numeral 8.

What does it mean, then, if you are constantly seeing 707, 808 or 909? The numeral 0 represents infinity and connection to the Christ Consciousness. If you see all of the above number sequences repeatedly it means that you are already a wayshower and a bridge for others to transcend the Galactic Gateway of the 8th chakra; you are a teacher of others. Well done if this applies to you – we are grateful for your assistance, as all angelic energy must be grounded through a human, physical body in order to be of service.

Once you have activated your etheric Lightbody through the Ascension Portal you will be anchored to the Crystalline Lightworker's Grid.* The energy in the grid will complete the final phase of the ascension process by streaming its energy into your etheric bodies. Once anchored to the grid you can send loving energy and healing to the world and into the Human Collective Consciousness at any time, whether you are consciously upon the grid or not.

When energy is sent from one Lightworker, it harnesses the energy from the entire grid, meaning that the impact of the healing upon the world is that of the Law of Group Endeavour. The power of this healing cannot be overestimated. If infused with the Violet Flame of Transmutation the negativity that is transformed to love will also be sent back to the world, which will be of great benefit to humanity.

Now is the time to take notice of the loving guidance around you and to become much more diligent in your spiritual practices. Take extra care that your thoughts and words reflect positivity and love, because any lower energies

Chapter 23

around you can only take hold if your energies match theirs. Bring in as much light as you can so you can enter the Ascension Portal and become a light for the world. Ask us, the Masters of Light, for assistance if so required.

    I AM Archangel Gabriel

*For more information on the Crystalline Lightworker's Grid read Chapter 9, "The Crystalline Grid,' p.39 in *The Alignment of the Universe: Messages from Other Worlds."* (Cochrane, 2015).

Meditation Twenty Three
Enter the Ascension Portal

Focus on your heart space and breathe consciously on a slow count of four breaths in and out, visualising light building in your heart space until it has totally surrounded you. Breathe in, breathe out, pushing the light further out around your body each time. At the same time, be aware of your feet grounded firmly on the floor.

Hold the intention that the four Archangels of Direction Archangels Michael, Uriel, Gabriel and Raphael surround you, using the Creator's energy to cleanse your aura, to ground you and to keep you protected through this meditation. Also hold the intention that they guide you to enter and go through the Ascension Portal and to anchor you onto the Crystalline Lightworker's grid, in the highest and best way, for your highest and best.

Stay centred, focusing on your breath as the Archangels balance and align your chakras, then bring them to a higher frequency of light in readiness for your Ascension activation in the portal.

When they are done, you will see, feel or imagine going above the Universe with the archangels towards a golden structure that has a pillar on each side. It is emitting a bright white/golden light. You join other human lightworkers in their etheric bodies streaming towards and into the portal. As you enter the portal, your etheric body turns golden and you will feel a rush of warm energy throughout your physical body.

Once you are through to the other side of the portal, you

join your fellow Lightworkers as you are all anchored to your vortex point on the Crystalline Grid. The Earth is below and encased in the grid that is alight with crystalline energy. As you find your place, the crystalline energy from the grid enters your feet and activates your crystalline Lightbody.

Now, looking below you, see the Earth. Holding the intention of sending the healing energy of the unconditional love of the Universe infused with the Violet Flame of Transmutation to all innocent people, into the human collective consciousness, to parts of the world that are suffering, or to plants, animals and trees that need help, project your light through the grid. It will immediately harness the energy of all Lightworkers around the world who are anchored into the grid. Watch as it is infused with violet light and ask that the healing is magnified one thousand times by the angelic realm and witnessed by the Masters of Light. Hold the energy until you feel a rush of energy back up through your body.

Cleanse the energy of the grid by bringing the light of Source through your crown chakra and sending it through your body into the grid. You will immediately see the light of the grid brighten. Bring the energy back up and wash your own energy off, then consciously bring your attention back into the room.

Break your energy from the healing by consciously breaking ties or asking Archangel Michael to do it for you. Ground your energy into the Earth and take a moment to centre your energy in your heartspace.

I AM Archangel Metatron.

Chapter 24
The Colours of the Ascension of Humanity

Colour is the fabric of the world. It is used by artists, illustrators, authors, actors, dancers and the media to portray emotions in a way that persuades the audience to respond in a certain way, or that communicates the reality of the story. Colour speaks in a way that the spoken word sometimes cannot do and is a powerful healing tool that is the study of some but overlooked by many.

The power of colour is that it holds healing properties within it that resonates with different parts of the body at different times and in different situations. This is because different shades of colour are a match for different emotions, feelings, states of mind and health and can be a healing modality for the person just by wearing that colour.

Consider, for a moment, the seven colours of the rainbow. The spectrum of colours within a rainbow rarely change when they appear, yet within each colour there can be many subtle shades. These colours are all one and the same with the light and love of the Creator because they are, of course, fractures of white light and thus pure in essence. Each colour in the spectrum holds its own vibration of energy that resonates with one of the seven angelic rays which are aligned to the chakras as well as to an Archangel. So, any colour that you are suddenly drawn to may be an indication that you are blocked in some way in that colour chakra; the angel aligned with it is the best one to call upon to help you to release the emotional blockage that is causing physical issues. This is possible because each chakra holds a pure vibration of light that, when at its highest and most vibrant, brings the person to optimum health, wellbeing and to be in perfect balance.

Just as the sky may seem more radiant with colour at sunrise and sunset, the hues of a rainbow are also becoming brighter to the eye. If one were truly observant, one would see a change in the tones and hues of colours that have become familiar. Yellows are now gold tinged with pink, blues are now more indigo, and greens are flecked with gold. These colours are a noticeable indication that change is happening within humanity and a mass awakening is indeed occurring, despite all attempts by darker forces to prevent it.

The colour pink represents love in all its forms. Rose pink is a deeper embodiment of love in that it represents budding and blossoming like a rose – an unfolding, if you like, petal by petal, until it is fully formed and complete. Gold is the colour of Christ, of a higher consciousness and of a higher order of Mastery. Rose gold, then is the embodiment of the Christ consciousness, which is mastery of love in all its forms and the transmission of teachings of a much higher order of consciousness.

To see rose gold emanating from the sky is a blessing because it is a sign that your world is transforming from darkness to light and you are shedding your third dimensional shell, thus emerging into the higher realms of consciousness. This colour shows that love is the unifying force of the Universe, connecting all living and non-living things as one in the energy of Source, the Creator of All That Is and that you are now embracing your true spirituality and stepping into the power of Who You Are.

If you see the colour violet or purple tinging the rose gold, this is a sure sign that Lightworkers and Starseeds are sending energy to transmute the lower vibrational frequencies emitted by unawakened, disconnected and disillusioned souls. These people will awaken in their own time but are, for now, being supported and encouraged by their guides through their respective journeys. They include those humans who wish to do harm for their own benefit. There is no judgement for their actions in the ethereal kingdom, for they must be their own judge and jury when it is time to review their life after their passing.

The colours of the ascension of humanity can be used to assist your own awakening and transition to the higher vibrational frequencies of the 5th

Chapter 24

dimension. If you focus on bringing more light into your chakras and energetic fields through meditation and gratitude, you may begin to notice the regular colours of your chakras deepening and changing in their hues. The higher their vibration the faster they turn, altering their frequency which is represented through colour. They will become iridescent and begin to take on the galactic colours of aqua, gold, magenta, deep violet and sparkling silver. Your etheric guides will become of a higher order and your ability to meditate and access your higher mind will increase. You may also find that your psychic senses will either activate or become heightened.

Colour contains frequencies of light, and when combined they become the iridescent white light of Creation. All paths lead to the light, so let colour lead you to find a higher vibration and connection to the God within and to your own Divinity.

We are the Cosmic Council, (formerly known as the Brotherhood of Light.)

Meditation Twenty Four
Align to the Rays of Ascension

Close your eyes and make yourself comfortable. Take a few, slow breaths in and out, being mindful of how your body is feeling. On each outbreath, feel your shoulders relaxing and your body becoming heavier in the chair.

Now gather your energy in your heartspace. It is a beautiful ball of energy, white and pearlescent with perhaps a tinge of blue. It rotates slowly and gathers in mass with each breath. Breathe in and out through your nose on a count of four, bringing in the light of the Creator into your energy ball on each inward breath, then breathing out stress and negativity.

Send your energy down through your chakras at the front of your body to your base, then feel the light separate down your legs and through your feet into the floor below. Imagine the two beams of light going down and anchoring deep into Mother Earth. Give thanks and blessings for all of her gifts, then bring the light back up through your feet and legs and back up through your chakras until your ball of energy is rotating slowly above your crown. Look up and see it. As you look you can see the beam of light that continues from your crown, through your own energy all the way through many more chakras to a much larger ball of energy. This is Creator's light, and you are directly connected to Him.

Now imagine yourself sitting in your own energy. You are surrounded by your own love and light. You feel immensely relaxed and peaceful. You feel yourself rising up and merging with the light of the Creator and becoming one with it. There is no separation between your light and

Chapter 24

Creator's light – you are simply One with all that is.

We call in now the master of light who is to work with each of you today to clear, balance, align and activate your chakras to bring a higher frequency of light into them, aligning them with the energies of Ascension. The master may be different for each person and the process shorter or longer, depending on the amount of light already present in each chakra and the frequency of light each person is able to tolerate. This process can take up to a minute and, for some, the energy can be quite strong. Rest assured you are safe and protected throughout this process and you will feel rejuvenated and calm afterwards. It is hoped you will find yourself more tolerant of others and more able to cope with the disrupted energies abounding on the Earth at this time.

Close your eyes and feel the master behind you. Ask for His/Her name or ask to be shown their colour. He/She has their hands gently on your head. The first wave of energy washes over you, clearing your aura and chakras of any discordant energies. It will also ground you more into the Earth. The next wave comes now, straightening your chakra line and balancing each chakra to allow them to receive a higher frequency of light. The energy ascends back up your body to prepare for the activation and then comes through for a third time. Feel the energy shifting throughout your body as the master of light activates your light frequencies to align to a higher level of consciousness and the 5th Dimensional energies of Ascension.

As He/She again grounds your energies, see, feel or imagine the light around you becoming brighter and lighter in essence. In your hands now receive a gift. It is a ball of light aligning you with the ray that you have been matched with. Notice, feel or know the colour, or ask to be told. As you place this ball of light in your crown and feel the chakra it relates to expand, open your mouth and emit a long tone three times. It will help the energy to integrate and align with yours.

Open your eyes and write down the first thing that comes to mind. Hear or know the message from the Master that is relevant to you at this time. Trust in your ability to do so.

You are very loved.

I AM Archangel Michael.

(Note: The chakras and associated rays:
1. Base chakra: 1st, Blue Ray, Archangel Michael and Lady Faith
2. Sacral Chakra: 5th, Green Ray, Archangel Raphael and Lady Mary
3. Solar Plexus: 3rd, Pink Ray, Archangel Chamuel and Lady Charity
4. Heart Chakra, 4th, White Ray, Archangel Gabriel and Lady Hope
5. Throat Chakra, 2nd, Yellow Ray, Archangel Jophiel and Lady Christine
6. Third Eye Chakra, 6th, Ruby Ray, Archangel Uriel and Lady Grace
7. Crown Chakra, 7th, Violet Ray, Archangel Zadkiel and Holy Amethyst)

Chapter 25
The Power of Meditation

Imagine in your mind a beautiful garden. It is the most peaceful and tranquil place you have ever been in. There are many shady trees on manicured lawns, flowers in well-kept gardens and water trickling in a stream under a bridge. Birds are singing and there are rabbits and other animals hopping around close by. A gentle breeze blows on your face, and the sun warms your feet. All is peaceful and your mind is empty as you revel in the beauty surrounding you. When you leave the garden you feel refreshed, relaxed and revived, ready to resume your day.

Meditation is as simple as this, Dear Ones. There are many people who say they cannot meditate and still their minds, yet when you sit and just 'contemplate your navel', as the saying goes you are essentially meditating! It can be as simple or as complicated as you like. There are no rules and no time limit – it can take one minute or twenty, five minutes or an hour. You can stare at a wall, walk on the beach, connect to the Creator or chant for the whole time. However you do it the purpose is always the same: to clear your mind, centre your spirit and connect to the ALL, which is also your connection to your Higher Self, your subconscious thoughts and your own self in Spirit. Spirituality, after all, is connection and meditation is the highest and best way to restore or maintain it.

There are many types of meditation, some of which are 'interactive', where contact with guides, spirits or the Creator is made. However, most people who meditate do so in order to centre themselves within their own Being, to make contact with the deep spirituality within and to increase their sense of health and overall wellbeing. In the rush of daily life, a multitude of thoughts run through peoples' minds at the same time, clouding the ability to see the bigger picture and to think clearly and rationally. It is very easy to become ungrounded and disconnected, to the world around you and to the spiritual voice within. Meditation is the best way to re-centre, re-ground and re-connect to yourself, Mother Earth, the Supreme Source and to your spiritual self.

Clearing your mind may seem difficult but having a focus may help. Some people use pre-recorded guided meditations, some play music, some use chanting or toning. Others focus on their breath or on a visualisation. There are many different ways, but it is recommended that you focus on your breathing while visualising it as light. As you breathe in light and fill every part of your body with it, you can imagine that it is renewing all of your cells, repairing tissue and reinstating your health. Such is the power of the mind that, as you imagine it happening, it will actually be happening! As you breathe out the light, breathe it out as love and hold the intention that it goes out to the world, to people you love, to people who need it or even to the Earth itself. Doing this is much more powerful than you could know.

The power of meditation is that it harnesses the power of the mind, in connection with the rest of your body, with the Supreme Source, Mother Earth and with the Universe itself. The mind is a powerful manifestor, but in lower or more fractured vibrations it can work in destructive, judgemental and quite detrimental ways. In the meditative state, it is much easier for the mind to be calm, connected to the ALL and free of attachments to the Earthly and Third Dimensional planes. Meditation allows the mind to be open to the messages that are available from the etheric planes and for natural psychic abilities to develop. Starting with the breath will immediately connect the meditator to their sacred fire, and the resulting connection to the ALL will be deeper, more profound and much more relaxing, particularly for the beginner.

In these troubled times, it is easy to feel weighed down with worry and despair. It is so hard to stay positive but, Dear Hearts, that is exactly what you must work hard to do, because the more positivity there is in the world, the higher the vibrational the energy emanating from the Earth and Humanity itself. This is important because energy creates more of the same energy, so the more people that extract themselves from the gloom of society, the easier it will be to bring in love and light to transform your reality. By making meditation part of your daily or regular practice you will find yourself more able to allow yourself to be more responsive and far less reactive to the dense energy around you. If every person in the world learned to meditate and practiced mindfulness, breathing and the simple act of sending love to the world, what a different place it would be!

Whether you focus on your breath, chant a mantra or listen to a visualisation, any form of meditation is beneficial. If you really find it difficult to shut your mind off, start with a minute a day and build up your stamina slowly. Persistence and practise are key.

Archeia Mary has a simple visualisation meditation for you to try.

Many blessings,

I AM Archangel Michael

Meditation Twenty Five
A Warm Hug Meditation

Close your eyes and make yourself comfortable. Take a few, slow breaths in and out and become mindful of how your body is feeling. On each outbreath, feel your shoulders relaxing and your body becoming heavier in the chair. Begin to focus on your breath, counting four breaths in and four breaths out until you have a regular rhythm. Breathe in, two, three, four and out, two, three, four. Breathe in, two, three, four and out, two, three, four. Focus entirely on your breath and on relaxing your body.

Now see, feel or imagine my energy around you as a warm and soft cloak made of the finest silk. The colour is pink turning to lilac and, as it wraps gently around your shoulders, it makes you feel completely safe. You now see, feel or imagine yourself sitting on soft grass on the bank of a beautiful lake, which is surrounded by reeds and wildflowers. You feel a soft breeze on your face and the sun is warm on your skin. The lazy buzz of insects makes you feel drowsy as you watch ducks swim. You see the odd frog hopping on lily pads, rabbits grazing nearby and hear birds singing sweetly in the trees.

The water is still and calm, the lake deep and the water is beautifully clear. As you watch the water, its calmness gives you an inner peace that you have not felt for a long time. In your mind's eye, you lay back and absorb the stillness into your being, wrapped in my cloak and surrounded by the simplicity of nature. Your breath has now slowed to six breaths in and six breaths out as you relax in this beautiful setting. Breathe in, two, three, four, five, six and out, two, three, four, five, six. Breathe out two, three, four, five, six and out, two, three, four, five, six.

Feeling totally peaceful, calm, safe and relaxed, bring your focus back to my energy which is still wrapped around you like a cloak. I am now sending healing to your physical, emotional, mental and spiritual bodies. As my energy soaks into your Being, you feel a rush of release from your chakras, aura and physical body, allowing negative energies to be replaced by love, light and the higher vibration of joy. Stay in this energy until you feel lighter, warm and uplifted.

I am now my lifting my cloak from your shoulders and you feel a strong grounding sensation as you gently come back to the room feeling peaceful, centred and very loved. You may call upon me at any time to repeat this meditation.

I AM Mother Mary (the Archeia of Archangel Raphael).

Chapter 26
Take Back Your Power and Embrace Your Mastery

When you were born your connection to Source was absolute. You could still see your angels and you played with the elementals around you. You possibly saw your passed-over relatives and knew you were always protected by the light.

As children grow, however, they can become disconnected from their psychic abilities and spiritual family through many influences such as religious indoctrination, abuse, neglect, family cultural traditions and so on. Belief in psychic abilities and the supernatural has aroused suspicion over the ages and, as has been well recorded, was punishable by death in the middle ages.

Whether you wish to be psychic or not, connection to the light of Source, or God, is not just a right for those who subscribe to religious doctrine or biblical beliefs. All souls living in a human body on Earth at this time are connected to the unconditional love of God the Creator and are therefore also connected to each and every other soul, not just on the planet but in the entire Universe. Separation is but a veil of illusion that you placed in your energy field long ago to allow your soul to experience all of the facets of life on Earth. Now, as the energies of Ascension accelerate and the veil is lifting more each day, humans are awakening to the reality of their own Divinity within their soul's blueprint. They are taking back their power as ethereal light-Beings and co-creators.

No longer must humans feel they are lesser than God or each other. In the energy of God, the Creator of All That Is, everything in the Universe is one and the same, created in a stillpoint of time with unconditional love. Love, therefore, is all there is and Love is the only thing that can bring life on Earth back into balance.

Now is the time for every person to embrace the changes that are happening upon the Earth and claim back their power and mastery as a co-creator of the Universe. Belief is the key here. When you can believe in the power of the mind, you can also believe in the power of the heart. When you can see beyond the limitations of life in a physical body, you will start to lift the veil of illusion that has been blocking your true vision; that of the third eye and your connections to the ethereal world. When you love, accept and believe in yourself you will embrace the changes that are happening within your Being and step into Who You Truly Are – you will embrace your mastery.

While there are many ascended masters walking the Earth through reincarnating into a human body, some find it too difficult to remain in such dense, heavy energy, both in the physical body and in a world that is so unjust. Many more have awoken, however, and have become wayshowers for others to traverse their own awakening. Achieving mastery in a human body is no mean feat. It is plagued with the difficulties of living life on a planet steeped in negativity, attachment to money, drama, illusions of grandeur and the inequal distribution of resources. It is not helped by inflated egos that use unfair means to get what they want. Wayshowers know only too well how diligent they must be in keeping their energies clear and their vibrations high in order to remain relatively unattached to the ego, drama and illusion of life on Earth. It is always a work in progress!

Mastery, or enlightenment, is about being able to live in the physical, third-dimensional world while always being aware of your connection to your spiritual guidance and the gifts that are available to you. However, there are plenty of people in the world who have mastered their gifts but have used them to plunder universal abundance for themselves at the expense of the free will and wellbeing of others around them. One can be a Master of Darkness just as easily as a Master of Light. Intention is the key here, coupled with faith, trust and total belief in one's abilities to create. With intent, it will be, but only when the intention creates in the energy of Love will one tread the true path of an

Chapter 26

Ascended Master of Light.

To reach the stage where your Ascended Lightbody has been activated and you are anchored to the Crystalline Grid as a Lightworker for the planet takes practice, motivation and diligence. Light activations must be integrated gradually so as not to overwhelm the physical body with too many higher frequencies that can cause disquieting physical symptoms. Along the way you must work on releasing all past trauma and blockages that have prevented you from forgiving yourself or others for past misdeeds. You must also learn to meditate so that you can find your connection to Source through the sacredness of your own divinity. People in the process of ascending to the Fifth Dimension often find themselves a mentor, someone who has been through the process themselves but who can also train them to connect to their own psychic gifts and spiritual purpose. Once on track, the person's guides will make themselves known and be of great assistance in their spiritual awakening and ongoing development.

Achieving a level of enlightenment that allows you to remain connected to Spirit while walking the Earth as a human being brings with it a certain level of responsibility to help others to experience the bliss of connecting to the Divine and standing in their power without shame or fear of judgement. It also allows the master to positively influence the world around them around the clock whether they are consciously intending to or not.

I AM Archangel Michael

A Final Word

Time passes according to the perspective of each person; for some it crawls by painfully slowly, but for others there are never enough hours in the day. Time is, however, an Earthly measure and does not, in universal language, exist at all. This moment in time is all that matters, for the past is over and the future is yet to come. Those who dwell on the past will often only succeed in blocking their future path; while the events and people of the past may have helped to shape who you are today, they do not represent your full potential. If events and people in your past have left unhappy and ugly memories, it is more important than ever to attempt, from the core of your being, to forgive them and yourself then to let it all go. It is very difficult to move forward when the past is anchoring you there.

Life on Earth is short and time does not wait for anyone. If you reflected on your life, how much of it has been wasted worrying about the actions of others, reliving trauma, stressing about the future or doing nothing at all? Do you appreciate your life as it is now, making the most of every minute as if it were a gift? Life on Earth IS a gift and much can be accomplished, if one acts mindfully, purposefully and from their heart.

Allow the past to rest and live for the moment, Dear Hearts, breath by breath, step by step, minute by minute, day by day. Acknowledge the lessons you have learnt, give thanks to those who have helped you to learn them and celebrate the strength and courage that has allowed you to be the person you are at this very moment. Embrace the gifts you have been given and use them to create a positive present and a future filled with possibilities. Live your life in the present and make the most of every moment with gratitude and love.

Open your heart and mind to the possibilities that are available to you. What you believe you create in divine union with the Creator of All That Is. Whether you know it or not, you are a spoke of the divine wheel that turns in unison with the vehicle of Creation. Every thought creates an action that causes events to unfold. The reactions to your actions in turn create more thoughts and more resulting actions. The wheel turns positively or negatively, depending on your mindset and your intention.

The world is full of beauty, yet there is so much ugliness upon her surface. Ugly thoughts lead to ugly words and deeds that are reflected in the environment around you. Once formed, negative thought forms stay within the universal consciousness, sometimes for many years, until they are cleared by lightworkers sending energy or by changes in mindset from the people who formed them. No deed can be entirely undone; however, there is much that can be done to reverse the effects of hatred, abuse, violence and retribution in an area of war, unrest or where large populations reside together.

We the masters cannot stress enough the importance of sending light and love to areas where there has been much killing and violence. The more people around who do this the more light will penetrate the darkness and the impetus of war will be slowed. You may not think that such an act can have such a powerful impact but, in a universe that exists on love alone, it is the only effect it can have.

Visualise the Earth and an area you wish to send love and light to. Connect your energy to the Creator, or Source, and hold the intention of love and light flooding the areas you are focusing on. Feel the peaceful effect that this energy is having on the people in the area, even if it is not at first apparent. With intent, it will be so. If many people participated in this one, simple act every day, the impacts would be noticeable.

Love is ALL there is. You are a part of the ALL and loved unconditionally.

And so it is.

WE ARE The Masters of the Cosmic Council.

Recorded Meditations

All meditations in this book have been recorded by Victoria and set to music by Gary Martin.

After purchasing this title, go to
https://victoriacochrane.com.au/meditations
and type in the code **BOL606**
to gain full access to all 25 recorded meditations.

All rights reserved.

Credits

Cover designed and drawn by Renea Stubbs, formatted by Synk Media

Recorded Meditations formatted and set to music by Gary Martin:

www.cosmotune.com;

www.facebook.com/Solfeggio-Sound-Healing

Music

Part 1 Meditations 1 -9 Daydreams. Purchased from Christopher Lloyd Clark, Enlightened Audio

Part 2 Meditations 10-20 Across the Sky. Purchased from Christopher Lloyd Clark, Enlightened Audio

Part 3 Meditations 21-25 A Pure Embrace. Purchased from Christopher Lloyd Clark, Enlightened Audio

Editing: Kelly Parker and Gary Martin

About the Author

Victoria Cochrane (M Ed. Hons) is the Tasmanian Psychic Expo's 2019 Tasmanian Psychic of the Year, a certified member of the International Psychic's Directory and regular presenter of The Spiritual Wisdom Hour on Spiritual Events and Directory's Facebook Page.

A trained Advanced Theta® Healing practitioner, Usui Reiki Master and author, Victoria uses her psychic clairvoyance, mediumship and channelling abilities to help people to lift their past trauma and limiting belief system to heal aspects of their lives in order to move forward. She also tutors people to step onto their own spiritual path, to connect to their guides and to embrace their own particular gifts.

Victoria writes a monthly newsletter *www.reachingoutspiritualnews.blogspot.com* and has a Facebook page of the same name. She also has a channellings blog *victoriacochrane44.com* where she publishes regular channelled messages from the masters. She has also collaborated with Gary Martin *www.cosmotune.com* on two moving light spectrum meditation albums. She can be seen each Wednesday at 12 Noon for her Spiritual Wisdom Hour on the Spiritual Events Directory's Facebook Page.

Victoria lives on the NW Coast of Tasmania with her husband Richard. They have 3 adult sons and a baby granddaughter. Victoria conducts appointments in her healing room in Wynyard, Tasmania, or via video call on Skype, WhatsApp or Messenger.

Victoria Cochrane: *Accurate, Compassionate, Life-Changing*

victoriacochrane.com.au

Other Titles by Victoria Cochrane

Raising the Energies of Mother Earth Towards and After Ascension 2012: The Highest Truth
2013, Victoria Cochrane Publications

Channelled entirely from the Masters of the Cosmic Council The 12/12/12 was the moment when Mother Earth ascended into a New Age, where man now has the opportunity to leave the old ways of living in ego and serving the self behind. The universe revolves around unconditional love. Man is part of the all and is one with, not separate from, God, the Creator of All That Is. We are all spiritual beings on an onward soul journey and most of us have lived many lives. The Earthly Plane is the stage where humans learn the lessons their souls have chosen to learn in order for their souls to evolve. Everything we do or that happens to us on Earth is either a result of a lesson we have chosen or the invocation of karma by us or by other souls.

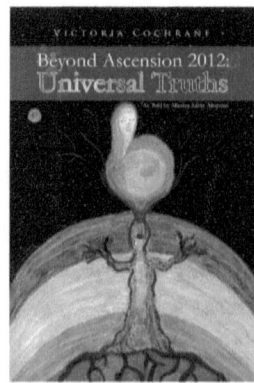

Beyond Ascension 2012: Universal Truths
2016 (2nd Edition), Victoria Cochrane Publications

Continues the theme of the first book and explains truths about humans as ethereal beings who are having a human experience in order to learn lessons towards soul growth and enlightenment. It explains how we live on planes of existence and are all bound by spiritual law. Master Aloysius also explains the significance of our dreams, how we astral travel when we are sleeping and the benefits of praying to God and meditation. The manifestation of past life trauma as physical illness, the journey of the soul, the planes of existence and universal laws are also explained. The energies of the newly ascended Earth into the Fifth Dimension has been deemed by Creator to be the right time for the Masters of the Fifth Plane to bring the truths of the universe, which are all based upon spiritual law, to man at this time. We are moving into a new age where the higher vibrations will no longer tolerate the darker energies of manipulation of truth, corruption, greed and inequalities of the Third Dimensional past.

The Alignment of the Universe, Messages from Other Worlds
2015, Victoria Cochrane Publications

On 21/12/12, after Mother Earth ascended, she came into alignment with several planets from other parts of the galaxy. Although over a year has passed since this momentous event, it has opened the way for these planets and their amazing, peaceful beings to communicate with us and to assist us to raise our vibrations as a race and to ascend with the Earth. It is in their own interest to do so, because, just as we on Earth are one with God and each other, so is the entire universe one. What occurs on Earth, therefore, affects all other living beings in the universe, and they have no desire to see us self-destruct.

Channelled from the Masters of Light and Members of the Inter-Planetary Galactic Federation, this book explains how human souls can learn from the lives of beings on other planets who are much more evolved than us. It is past time for us to listen.

Light Source Meditations
A Relaxing Journey into the Light (DVD, 2017, Victoria Cochrane and Gary Martin). Available from *victoriacochrane.com.au* and *www.cosmotune.com*

Dimensions of Light
Meditative Journeys (2020, Available from *victoriacochrane.com.au* and *www.cosmotune.com*

www.ingramcontent.com/pod-product-compliance
Lightning Source LLC
Chambersburg PA
CBHW030256010526
44107CB00053B/1738